MAGGIE ALPHONSI

WINNING THE FIGHT

WITH GAVIN MAIRS

POLARIS
PUBLISHING

This edition first published in 2025 by

POLARIS PUBLISHING LTD
c/o Aberdein Considine
2nd Floor, Elder House
Multrees Walk
Edinburgh
EH1 3DX

www.polarispublishing.com

First published in 2023
Text copyright © Maggie Alphonsi and Gavin Mairs, 2023, 2025

ISBN: 9781915359346
eBook ISBN: 9781915359025

The right of Maggie Alphonsi and Gavin Mairs to be identified as the authors of this work has been asserted by them in accordance with the Copyright, Designs and Patents Act 1988.

All rights reserved. No part of this publication may be reproduced, stored or transmitted in any form, or by any means electronic, mechanical, photocopying, recording or otherwise, without the express written permission of the publisher.

The views expressed in this book do not necessarily reflect the views, opinions or policies of Polaris Publishing Ltd (Company No. SC401508) (Polaris), nor those of any persons, organisations or commercial partners connected with the same (Connected Persons). Any opinions, advice, statements, services, offers, or other information or content expressed by third parties are not those of Polaris or any Connected Persons but those of the third parties. For the avoidance of doubt, neither Polaris nor any Connected Persons assume any responsibility or duty of care whether contractual, delictual or on any other basis towards any person in respect of any such matter and accept no liability for any loss or damage caused by any such matter in this book.

Every effort has been made to trace copyright holders and obtain their permission for the use of copyright material. The publisher apologises for any errors or omissions and would be grateful if notified of any corrections that should be incorporated in future reprints or editions of this book.

British Library Cataloguing-in-Publication Data
A catalogue record for this book is available on request from the British Library.

Designed and typeset by Polaris Publishing, Edinburgh
Printed in Great Britain by MBM Print SCS Limited, East Kilbride

CONTENTS

FOREWORD	vi
PROLOGUE	1
ONE: Punching my weight	7
TWO: My rebel yell	15
THREE: Defying the odds	25
FOUR: The crusading Saracen	31
FIVE: Finding Maggie	40
SIX: Falling from the top of the world	51
SEVEN: Seven heaven	59
EIGHT: World in motion	66
NINE: Maggie the Machine	72
TEN: We are not men	83
ELEVEN: Portacabin dreamin'	88
TWELVE: Breaking Good	95
THIRTEEN: The tipping point	105
FOURTEEN: 'Doctor of Rugby'	117
FIFTEEN: The state of the union	134
SIXTEEN: Winning the fight	142
SEVENTEEN: The Troublemakers	154
EIGHTEEN: 'Thank you, Miss'	166
NINETEEN: Top of the Pops	182
TWENTY: The Long Shot	193
TWENTY-ONE: Owning my voice	205
TWENTY-TWO: My greatest achievement	220
TWENTY-THREE: Rebel with a cause	232
ACKNOWLEDGEMENTS	245

To my wife, Marcella, our children Artie and Willow, and my mum, Rebecca. You mean everything to me. And to my extended family Christine, Kevin, Siobhan, Jon and Annabel. Thank you for your love and support.

'Be Comfortable, being uncomfortable'
Peter McWilliams

'If it doesn't challenge you, it won't change you'
Fred Devito

FOREWORD

BY SIR CLIVE WOODWARD

I think I managed to hugely embarrass Maggie the first time we worked together at ITV. 'I used to come and watch you play,' I told her. 'No, you didn't, surely not,' she replied in a self-deprecating manner that belied her status as one of England's greatest players of all time.

But the truth is that I had always admired her as a player from afar. I told her that I used to go to England matches simply to watch her in action. That's sport. We all love certain players in different teams. A player who we want to see get the ball or make a big tackle. When I watch the Saracens men's team play, I like to focus on Owen Farrell. When I watched England Women, I watched Maggie Alphonsi. She was such a disruptive player, I found her utterly compelling.

She is a player I would love to have coached. I would put her in the same bracket as Farrell and Maro Itoje, players from the current era I know I would get on with and could get the best out of.

Maggie, like Owen and Maro, was what I call a 'sponge' player. Players who listen and soak up information but are also not 'yes' people either.

I was lucky to have a number of players like that when I was head coach of the England men's team that won the Rugby World Cup in 2003, such as Martin Johnson and Neil Back. They knew that if something made sense to them, they would just do it. Maggie had a mindset similar to Johnno, always learning, improving her skillset and underpinning it all with a ferocious physicality and commitment to put her body on the line for England. I can pay her no greater compliment.

I have seen her tackle Gareth Thomas in the ITV studio when we've done tackling drills and the impact was shuddering. Yet she did it all with a smile on her face. It was priceless TV. I can only imagine what it must have been like to come up against her on the pitch.

What is also remarkable about Maggie is her mental resolve and resilience. I know how tough it is to win a Rugby World Cup. We were well beaten by South Africa in the quarter-finals in 1999 and had to make significant changes going into 2003 in the way we played. Maggie played in two World Cup finals, losing both, before finally and gloriously lifting the trophy at the third attempt. Lesser players might have opted to take an easy path when the going got tough. But by the time of England's final in 2014, her determination to finish her career with a winner's medal had only intensified, not diminished. One of my favourite quotes is by the former South African president Nelson Mandela who said: 'I never lose. I either win or I learn.' Maggie learnt and found the way to win.

It was England's victory in 2014, and Maggie's central role in the triumph, that provided the springboard for the exciting growth in women's rugby that we are now seeing. She remains at the forefront of blazing a trail for women's sport and fighting for equality and greater opportunity for people from ethnic minorities, as a council member for the Rugby Football Union and through her media work and leadership talks.

Working alongside her for ITV has given me an insight into her rugby knowledge. When she first started, I would find myself asking her questions to try to bring her into the conversation.

'What do you think, Maggie?' I would ask her. Sometimes she looked at me as if to say, 'Thanks a lot!' but I wasn't trying to throw her a hospital pass. Having seen her play, I was intrigued to hear her point of view, both from a female perspective and from her deep knowledge of forward play, particularly the back row. She performs her role as a pundit in the same way as she did as a player: she has always got something to say.

I think she would make a magnificent coach. If we want to develop women's sport, we should be appointing females to coaching jobs, because it is the coach who gets the most airtime. Look at how well Sarina Wiegman has done with the Lionesses football team. She was appointed by Dame Sue Campbell, the FA's director of women's football. It is not until we have women in decision-making roles that we will see more female coaches.

Which is why Maggie's work to improve diversity and inclusion in rugby is so important. She was a pioneer as a player and now is continuing that fight as an administrator and by showing visible leadership through her media work. I can only wish her well. Knowing Maggie, she will not stop until the fight is won.

PROLOGUE

I could tell from the look in Owen Farrell's eyes that he wasn't going to pass the ball. He may have been just eighteen years old, but the future captain of the England men's team already looked the part, sporting a Justin Bieber-style floppy quiff. I'm sure he regrets it now. But even back then he had an aura about him. Everyone knew that his father was Andy Farrell, the rugby league legend who'd decided to finish his playing career in rugby union, for Saracens and briefly for England. But Farrell junior was the future now. And he knew it.

His teammates no doubt probably thought he was a bit up himself, but I could tell his overly confident demeanour wasn't misplaced. He was a player going places, and quickly. And he had no intention of letting me get in his way. It didn't matter to him that he was training against a woman – he quite rightly saw me as nothing more than an opposition player with a weakness that he would find and ruthlessly exploit. All he needed to do was make the pass, but I think when he saw that I was the defender he thought: 'I'm just going to run at her.'

I knew who his dad was too. But, on that freezing Tuesday night at the University of Hertfordshire grounds in Hatfield, I knew I only had one job. Ringing in my head was the phrase I'd heard, over and over again, from Geoff Richards, a tough-talking former Australia full-back who had been instrumental at the start of my international playing career during his time as head coach of the England women's side: 'Make the f**king tackle, Maggie; make the f**king tackle.'

****

If I knew who Owen's dad was, he certainly didn't know anything about me. *Why would he?*

It was March 2009 and Farrell was the rising star in the Saracens academy that was being compared to rugby union's equivalent of Manchester United's legendary Class of '92 that included David Beckham, Nicky Butt, Ryan Giggs, Gary Neville and Paul Scholes. Saracens' equivalent was similarly sprinkled with stardust; Farrell's teammates included future England and Lions forwards Jamie George and George Kruis, as well as Jackson Wray and Will Fraser, who would go on to play in the Premiership and in Europe.

They were all thriving as part of an uncompromising regime headed up by an equally uncompromising Eddie Jones. The future England head coach was in charge of Saracens then, and that night I was also given a unique insight into his forthright and challenging approach that would ultimately cost him his job with the national side more than a decade later.

To be fair to Eddie, he'd welcomed me into the fold. At the start of the 2008/09 season, the Rugby Football Union for Women (or the RFUW, as it was known until we merged with the RFU in 2010) had felt that the England Women's squad would benefit from taking part in training with the club academies from the men's game. As I already played with the Saracens' women side – along with veteran internationals Amy Garnett and Karen

Andrews – I'd been invited to take part in the training session with the Saracens academy. There was just one condition. When the coaches asked Eddie if it was okay for me to take part in the session, he said: 'Yes, it's fine but she's got to do everything that the boys do, though.'

I had no problem playing against the boys. In my wilder, childhood years, I'd squared up and fought against boys much tougher than that Saracens bunch on the patch of ground at the back of my block of flats in the Edmonton estate in north London, where I grew up. It was just the way of life back then. You had to stand your ground, even for those of us like me who didn't join a gang, whether you were a boy or a girl, because reputation was more important than your gender.

I'd also developed a bit of a relationship with the lads because I'd been to a few sessions before, and they appreciated that I was there to develop my skills. The problem was that on the very night that Eddie turned up, neither Karen nor Amy had been able to make it. I was on my own.

I travelled to the sportsground already in my kit so there was no awkwardness about changing before training, but I can remember getting out of my car and thinking: 'Do I really want to do this?'

Rugby players, men and women across the country will recognise the feeling. One of those nights when you don't fancy it. But as I knew I was the only woman turning up, I knew I had to. There was a burning ambition too. This was the sort of opportunity that I knew was special and that if I wanted to develop my game and progress further I had to do it.

I kept talking myself up as I slowly pulled on my boots: 'I can do this; I can do this.' When I saw Eddie was there too, I knew my reputation and that of the women's game was also on the line. *Come on Maggie, you've got this.*

****

It was a bloody hard session. Lots of running, a lot of hitting the floor and getting up again. If anyone dropped the ball, our punishment was to do some laps of the artificial pitch. I was embedded as one of them. In a weird way it was a good thing I was the only woman that day because I knew I had to step up and be visible – and I *wanted* to step up.

The tackling sessions were no problem. It might be hard to understand if you're a woman who has never tackled a man or a man who has never tackled a woman on the rugby pitch, but I'd been used to playing against some really big and physical women so I knew I could look after myself.

When people meet me nowadays for the first time, quite often they will comment on how small they think I am. And I grew up wanting to be like players such as Selena Rudge, who played for Wasps and won forty-seven caps for England. She was so strong and combative, like a mixed martial arts fighter blessed with rugby skills who would never take a backward step. Put it this way, you would never want to get into a ring with her. And she had thighs like Joe Cokanasinga, the Bath and England centre. When I tried to tackle her, it was like trying to stop a bus, she would pretty much run people over.

I was twenty-six when the RFUW had us train with the Saracens academy, so tackling eighteen-year-old men didn't strike me with any fear.

But Farrell was big for his age. He was taller and had a way bigger stature than me. The drill was three attackers versus two defenders. The defenders were outnumbered but had to make the right decision and make the tackle. When Farrell received the ball, it was my turn to defend. *Make the tackle Maggie. Make the tackle.*

He had one player outside him. He ran at me hard. I lined him up, with the perception that he was going to pass, but in the moment, I knew that he had no intention of passing. I can understand why.

But of all my abilities on the rugby pitch, tackling was my core strength. It had been drilled into me from my first days in rugby. It would go on to earn me the nickname 'Maggie the Machine' for my defensive work in the World Cup final in 2006, coined by former England internationals, Stuart Barnes and Dewi Morris who were on commentating duties that night when the game was broadcasted live on Sky Sports.

Before every tackle I made, I would always run through my options. *Do I go low and just make the leg tackle?* But that felt too risky. What if he stepped me? *Do I hit him near the hips?* But there was risk involved in that too, as he could simply offload to the extra attacker. No, there was only one option. I was going to have to go for man and ball. Literally. It may not have been the most amazing tackle in the world, but I remember hitting him and, in the collision, stopping him in his tracks before grabbing and pulling him down in the tackle.

I still remember to this day the coaches on the sidelines gasping: 'Oh my God, she has just taken down Owen Farrell.' The other lads loved it too.

The assumption was that Owen wasn't too happy about being tackled. Owen should have passed, and he didn't run at me again.

But at the time there was no other major reaction. I'd just done my job. I was meant to have made the tackle, just like Geoff Richards would have wanted. When you're with the lads, you just get on with it. There was no pat on the back. The reality was that I'd been supposed to make the tackle. All I cared about was not missing it. *That one was for you, Geoff.*

****

Looking back now I recognise that session as one of the defining moments of my career. I wanted to step out of my comfort zone and, in the moment, I'd stepped up. I learned something about myself that night and grew from it.

To have executed the tackle in front of Eddie Jones made it all the more special. He's not renowned for giving out praise.

When I used to talk to some of the Saracens men's players back then and England players when he was coach of the men's national side about their experiences of playing for Eddie, it mirrored my memories of him. He doesn't say many words, he's very to the point and he has a massive presence for a small man. I knew who he was, I knew what his history was and what he was going through with Saracens at the very time, but he only said a few words. Instead, you could find his judgement in his facial expression and his eyes. It made you feel you had to go out of your way to impress him.

But in the feedback from the session to the RFUW he said the words that I desperately wanted to hear: 'She fitted in like she was one of the lads. She did well.'

I'm not sure Owen or Eddie remember the moment now, but it stayed with me for the remainder of my career. Nowadays when I meet Eddie, I still have no idea if he knows it was me who made the tackle that night.

But on that Tuesday night in Hatfield, I felt I'd earned his respect. Owen's too, and the respect from the other lads who were in attendance that night. It was another staging post for me and left me with a feeling that fired me on through the highs and lows of my career.

I just remember thinking that night, not for the first time, 'I'm just going to be one of the lads. I'm going to train harder, run harder and tackle harder than any of them. There's no gender. I'm going to stand my ground and never take a backward step.'
You don't mess with Maggie. Even if you're a boy.

ONE

PUNCHING MY WEIGHT

The first time I felt invincible was the first time I got into a fight with a boy. And I managed to hit him. *Twice*. His name was Ian and I hit him hard, in his torso. And followed it up with another blow. I knew immediately from the look in his eyes that my blows had landed and hurt him.

Amid the flurry of fists and cheers from the crowd that had gathered around us, it was in that moment that I first became aware of my strength. It was exhilarating. I felt dominant and powerful and alive; a heady mix of emotions that I would come to love years later in a setting I couldn't ever have imagined on that hot afternoon in north London: playing rugby union for England.

My physical enlightenment instead took place on the patch of ground where I used to play football after school, the playing fields behind the block of flats in Edmonton, in north London. Football was king in my estate. No one ever talked about rugby. You were Spurs or Arsenal and I was one of the few girls who the boys didn't mind taking part in the after-school matches.

I'd deliberately chosen to fight Ian to make a point. We were both thirteen years old. Fighting was a rite of passage for kids growing up in the estates in Edmonton.

It wasn't a gang thing. Well, not in my case anyway. Despite the fact that my mother, as a single parent, had to work long hours – sometimes juggling two jobs at a time to raise me – she made sure I had a strict Nigerian upbringing. Yet, like every kid in the area, I had known that the day would come when I'd have to prove that I could look after myself. *This was that day.*

The fight took place after school. We were both smart enough to do it on neutral ground out of the sight of any teachers, and I knew that mum was still at work – she never got home before 7.30 p.m. – so there was no danger that she'd see us from the window of our two-bedroomed flat, where she still lives today.

Mum would have been furious with me if she knew what I'd got myself into, but it was she who had unwittingly led me to this point. As a child I had generally been submissive, apologising to everyone for everything and it had made me a soft target for bullying.

It had all changed the day Mum asked if I wanted to go to the shops at the bottom of our flat to buy some sweets. Life at times on the estate was challenging. There were people who I would see and think: *I really don't want to grow up and be like that person.* Clusters of people would hang out around the estate. Some sat in their flat all day playing loud music.

I'd been told to never answer the door to our flat when I was on my own or speak to anyone and I didn't feel comfortable going out at night.

But sometimes the threats came in daylight too, as I was about to find out. As I ran down the stairs, I bumped into a girl called Sonia, who went to my school and was a couple of years older than me.

'When you come back, I'm going to beat you up,' she said, with cold menace. I didn't understand what I'd done to her. She was big, white, had dark blonde short hair and wore thick glasses but it didn't cross my mind that her threat could have been racially motivated. And I'm pretty sure it wasn't.

Sonia had picked on me before, but it had never really bothered me and, as I headed to the shop, I hoped that she'd lose interest in me by the time I returned. This time she hadn't.

Sonia wasn't athletic, but she was a big strong girl, a lot bigger than me at the time, and I took quite a beating. When I got back to my flat, my mum was horrified. And angry.

Mum may have been strict, but she has always supported me, and this was the first time I'd seen her reveal her emotions. Sonia lived in our building on a different level and Mum went to her flat and I could hear her unleash a barrage of words at Sonia and her mum.

'Don't ever let anyone bully you or pick on you,' she instructed me when she returned. 'You have to always stand up for yourself in this world. You can't let people walk all over you.'

In a very different way, Mum that day had revealed herself to be a fighter too, even if it wasn't in the physical sense. And from that day on I vowed never to let anyone dominate me again.

She couldn't have known it, but Mum's reaction that day awoke a rebellious streak in me that had, up to that point, been held in check by my strict, religious upbringing.

I didn't actually hang out with anyone who deliberately looked to get into fights, or didn't join any gangs. But from that day on, I would never again take a backward step. If anyone started on me, I'd retaliate. If you wanted a fight, you'd get one.

****

And now Ian was getting one. He'd been angling for a scrap with me but by taking him on I was setting the bar high: if I could hold my own, my reputation would be secured. The message in the corridors of Salisbury School would be: 'Don't mess with

Maggie'. Ian was black, had trimmed hair and was about 5ft 6ins. He didn't need to worry about his reputation because his sister *was* in a gang at our rival school, Edmonton County.

As I wrestled him to the ground, he threw punches back at me. But fighting a boy wasn't a problem for me. I'd never seen any difference between boys and girls. I'd never been a *girly* girl. We were all just kids in my mind.

I'm pretty sure Ian felt that same way. He probably would have been bossed around at home by his sister, as she was quite a hard lady, so gender mattered little for him when it came to fighting. The only thing that mattered was to prove that you were hard, that you could look after yourself. It didn't matter if you were a boy or a girl, if someone started on you, you gave it back.

I managed to land at least two decent punches and the scuffle finally ended when someone pulled us apart. It had been a fair fight. There was no winner, but that mattered little to me.

My reputation was now secure. The word went around that I had been in a fight with Ian – *yes, Ian whose sister is in a gang* – and from then on everyone knew that I could look after myself. From then on, I appreciated my physical strength. My popularity grew. Ian and I eventually became friends.

If I ever see him when I get back to Edmonton to visit my mum, we have a laugh about that day when everything changed for me. From now on everyone knew: *You don't mess with Maggie. Even if you're a boy.*

****

One of the wonderful things about my upbringing was the mix of people who lived in my building. In the twenty-two floors, there were families with an African or Caribbean background, Turkish and Greek families, and about a fifth were white; a melting pot that ensured that race wasn't an issue. Some were unemployed and hung around the estate, but it wasn't all doom and gloom, there was an air of affluence too, with the smart cars in the car park acting as an inspiration for me to work hard.

Despite everything, there were people who were aspirational, regardless of the area they lived in, and you knew they were going to make it in life. I had one good friend called Jo who went on to play football for Tottenham Ladies. At my school there was also a big emphasis on drama and some pupils went on to feature in the iconic BBC children's soap, *Grange Hill*. I remember one girl called Joanne who spoke so beautifully it was as if she'd been to acting school rather than a tough comprehensive school in Edmonton. She was so glamorous as well. I kept thinking: 'This is not the school for you.'

Then one day our school newsletter came out and it said that Joanne was going to be featuring in *Grange Hill*. I ran home from school and put the television on. You had to look closely, because it turned out that Joanne was just an extra, but I remember feeling so proud seeing her in the background. And she even had a couple of lines.

There was another guy at my school who was remarkably talented at music. He was the kind of guy who helped the teachers put the musical productions together. He was from a Somalian background and could play any instrument he touched. I remember telling him that he was so talented, but he was so humble with it. Nowadays he is choreographing choirs and music productions.

One of my best friends, Athos, who I was in a band with when we were young, has gone on to make music that is frequently played on BBC Radio Six. I just loved the fact that, even though we weren't from a privileged background, there was a sense not only of belonging but also of many people wanting to get on – and some of them made it to the top. Later I would look at them and think to myself, 'I can do it too.'

My eagerness to participate in sport helped to mask the fact that I'd been born with a club foot (medically known as talipes) and, despite undergoing an operation as a baby, I still walked with a slight limp.

I was conscious of my limp, but no one else seemed to notice and regardless of my physical ability I still wanted to play sport. I was often the goalkeeper at breaktime when I played football with the boys. No one wanted to be the keeper, so the boys seemed happy with that. But my desire to prove myself was starting to get me into trouble. My reputation as a girl who could handle herself was gaining momentum. It might have made me popular in school but not with my teachers. Or the police.

I had too much energy, I was putting socialising ahead of my studies and it was starting to feel like every day ended with a telling off from my head of year or even the headmaster.

The submissive and apologetic girl who had discovered her rebellious self was suddenly – and very quickly – running out of chances.

In the end, it was a fight against a girl called Beatrice that forced me to change my ways.

I don't remember what started it or why we fell out, but by then when people on my estate heard I was in a fight, they would back me. It was great for me but it must have been so intimidating for my opponent.

Looking back, it should never have led to a fight. It was a silly argument that got out of hand because a crowd gathered and egged us on.

This time, unlike the fight with Ian, I ended up quite badly hurt. In the tussle her nails caught my face and left a deep cut across my right cheek, from my cheek bone to my lip.

When I got back to our flat, Mum was so worried that she called the police and the situation escalated when we realised that Beatrice's parents had done the same. The police arrived and spoke to all of us, including our parents and Beatrice's younger sisters.

Bringing shame on my Mum was the turning point. I realised that I was just an immature child. There had been no need to fight. Beatrice had been a friend and yet here we were, in trouble with the police and blood was oozing down my cheek. Seeing the police speak to Beatrice and her young sisters hit a nerve with me. I'd got what I'd deserved.

I thought: *I don't need this, I don't need to fight, why am I fighting? What is this achieving?*

I knew I had to change. I was quite a switched-on kid, but while I was bad outside of school I was really, really bad in school. It was creating tensions with my mum, who knew how important it was that I worked hard and made the best of my ability.

Yet my time was running out. At Salisbury School there was a disciplinary procedure for pupils who got into trouble. A green report card meant that you had to go to see your head of year at the end of the day to review your behaviour. A yellow report card escalated the issue and the worst report card of all was a red one, which meant you had to see the headmaster at the end of the day – and if your negative behaviour continued you'd be excluded from school.

It wasn't long after I'd received the red report card that I knew things couldn't go on as they were. It was a chance conversation with Liza Burgess, one of our PE teachers, that would change everything. I can still remember seeing her arrive in school sporting a black eye.

I was wandering the school corridors when we bumped into each other.

'Why have you got a black eye, miss?' I asked, transfixed.

'I was playing rugby on the weekend for Saracens.'

I was immediately impressed. 'No way . . .'

'Do you know what, Maggie? I think you could be really good at this sport. You're fit and strong and I think you'd love the physical nature of the game. Why don't you turn this energy into a positive and give the game a go?'

I don't know why I listened to her. I didn't have a habit of listening to teachers back then. I guess it was because I respected Miss Burgess and I loved sport and the fact that she was praising me at a time when all the others were criticising me all combined to strike a chord.

I didn't know that Miss Burgess was also captain of the Wales Women's rugby team and would later go on to teach future England stars Mako and Billy Vunipola at a school in Wales. I didn't know what she saw in me, and I certainly didn't know anything about rugby, but she must have seen my potential.

I'd grown up in a single-parent family on a football-obsessed council estate. I'd been born with a club foot and walked with a limp. I was a girl. I was black. There simply weren't many people like me who played rugby, or any top-level sport at all. But Liza didn't care about my excuses. She told me to go to Saracens (a bus journey away via the W6), which was my nearest rugby club that had a women's and girls' section and try it out. So, I did. Everything I ever knew about sport was about to change. Thankfully my life was too.

TWO

MY REBEL YELL

I can't tell you when my father left my mum. It was before I was born, and I have never met him. My mum, Rebecca, never chose to talk about him. All I know is that she met him after leaving Nigeria to come to England to study and work. I can understand, given that he had walked out on her and returned to Nigeria, leaving Mum to raise me by herself, why she is so reluctant to talk about him.

Growing up, knowing that he walked out on my mother, I actually didn't want to know anything about him, but annoyingly I was still intrigued and had a nagging interest to learn more about him. I remember wanting to ask Mum about his background but knew she didn't want to talk about him, so I didn't pry. The result is that I know nothing about him and grew up not knowing who he was. I don't hold any regrets, though. Given the way he left us, he doesn't deserve to be part of my or my mother's life, so I have no compulsion to try to track him down now.

What I did know was that Mum was a strong and independent woman. She still lives in Edmonton, and I find it hard at times going back to visit her. I love seeing her, but the memories of growing up on that council estate and still seeing the deprivation there does upset me.

Remembering my roots are important to me and it was those formative years living there that shaped my character – it's just hard seeing a place where you grew up not change despite it being almost two decades since I last lived there. It's like it's stood still in time, whilst everything around it has moved on.

My mother's story has been a remarkable one. She originally lived in Abuja, the capital of Nigeria, where she had two children – my half-brother Azeez and half-sister Latoya – with her first husband as part of a large wider family. But after a family dispute, she was pretty much pushed to leave the country and develop a life of her own in the UK. Her children were in their late teens, but she came under intense pressure from her family to stay and be a 'good wife'. She didn't want to leave, but she had no choice.

Azeez and Latoya never came over to England and I never got the chance to meet them. I did manage to maintain a long-distance relationship with Azeez via phone calls from Nigeria each week, as he had a good relationship with Mum. But it was a different story with Latoya. She and Mum didn't speak and subsequently I've never had any contact with her, and I still know nothing about her life. It does feel weird to have such an estranged family, but it was beyond my control.

Sadly, Azeez passed away before I could meet him. I remember coming back from England rugby duty in France and my mother saying the words I had dreaded to hear. 'Azeez has died.'

Seeing my mother drop to the floor on her knees and breakdown in tears is an image that still haunts me to this day. It was heart-breaking. Her child had passed and she wasn't able to be there to protect him.

The details surrounding his death still remain unclear to me, but he had died due to injuries sustained after a violent attack he experienced while travelling home in Nigeria. Still till this day, my biggest regret will always be not going over to Nigeria to meet him. I envy my friends who have siblings. Growing up, I always wished I could see mine. I craved the family bond and relationship many of my friends had with their brothers and sisters but unfortunately my life had not panned out that way.

I've been lucky to have a loving relationship with Mum, but I imagine it's different to what I perceived my friends had with their parents. She's always been there for me, and she was incredibly loving, but I think it was very much a typical African/Nigerian relationship in the sense that she expected me to just get my head down, work hard, not misbehave and didn't see the benefit in any extracurricular activities outside of school life.

I would see my friends go on holiday together and have lots of positive conversations about their lives, whereas, in contrast, I didn't always feel comfortable about opening up to her about a lot of stuff because we just didn't have that relationship. My Mum wasn't the sort of person to take me out to museums or theme parks. I think she was just repeating the strict African upbringing that she had herself.

****

We lived on the fifth floor of a twenty-two-storey block of flats, the main building that was surrounded by smaller flats and council houses; a typical north London estate. Families living on top of each other, kids hanging out in the parks in the area or by the local parade of shops.

My bedroom was a typical kid's room and just the right size for me as a young girl growing up. Garfield the cat and Thomas the Tank Engine were my favourite characters and would feature on my wallpaper and bed covers at various times when I was young.

I don't like the term 'tomboy' but I was quite gender neutral – I didn't play with dolls but I didn't play with tractors either. One of the benefits of living in a flat is that other children could come over regularly to play, which meant I didn't need a room full of toys. A little television and a Nintendo were all I needed.

Like most other children on the estate, I was raised in a single-parent family. Indeed, looking back, it was rare to see a family with both parents in that environment. But, in many ways, at times we were like one big family. And I just loved the diversity of the community. It was such a mix – around a third would have been black and from African/Caribbean backgrounds, probably a similar number of Turkish and Greek people and the rest were English and Caucasian.

It was so enriching to grow up in such a diverse community. Differences became normal and I had friends from every background. No one judged you for how you looked or spoke. The first time I really felt black and exposed to racism was when the Stephen Lawrence murder took place in 1993. That really hit home. Until that moment I'd never thought about race or that there were people who might dislike you because of the colour of your skin.

The old African proverb says it takes a village to raise a child. In north London, Mum certainly needed help with me. I didn't appreciate at the time what an effort she made to raise me by herself without any family support. I remember having weekly visits from a social services worker, who would provide support and advice to my mum as she struggled to raise me on her own. Often, she worked two jobs at the same time just to ensure that she could make ends meet and pay for childcare.

When I was really young, she worked as a cleaner but then progressed to work for the Nigerian High Commission as a secretary in the Nigerian Embassy. Balancing work commitments with raising a daughter meant that I had a lot of babysitters to look after me.

My main babysitter was a lady called Pearl, who has since passed. She had two sons and two daughters but was also a childminder and would look after up to five children at a time.

When I was a child, Mum would drop me off at Pearl's house on her way to work and pick me up in the evening. Pearl would walk us to school and then be at the school gates at the end of the day to pick us up again.

It was an unusual relationship as Pearl became something of a second parent, but not one I have fond memories of. She was strict and I feared her. Thankfully, the other children in her care were of similar age to me so were great companions; they became like brothers and sisters to me and made my time in her care a bit more pleasant.

We all used to assemble at a collection point after school – usually the playground at my infant or primary school and then walk back together to her house. Her kids were adults and lived at home, and we would frequently see them upon our return from school while we waited for our respective parents to pick us up.

As Mum worked in London, in the city, I was always the last one to be collected. Often, she did not arrive until after 8 p.m. I always loved it when she arrived, I couldn't wait to get out of that house, but the lesson that I learned from those formative years was about independence. It became okay not to have someone to rely on, but to look out for yourself, which would serve me well later on the rugby field.

It was always tough when we had productions or performances at school and the parents were invited to watch. Mum could never come, and after a while it was just something I came to accept. It was just hard seeing my friends being embraced by their family members after a production, while I had no one and just walked back to the classroom to be the only one in there waiting for everyone to return.

Raising me all by herself was a remarkable achievement, and while she had to be absent from many of my school activities, Mum always tried to make sure she provided for me, even though she never held down a high-paying job.

Often, we had to make do, however. I had no concept of her financial constraints. I tried to copy my friends' hobbies; we could just about afford guitar lessons but could not stretch to a piano or piano lessons. Pragmatism was key: if we can't do A, then let's do B. That was my normal.

****

Religion was also a major part of my early years. Mum was a really strict Christian so throughout my childhood from about the age of eight she would take me to St Edmund's Catholic Church at the bottom of Bounces Road. Rather than let me go to Sunday School, Mum insisted that I sit with her in church, both of us dressed in our Sunday best.

Some of my mum's friends were also very religious – Nigerian people generally are – and while I didn't go to a faith school, it was part of my life.

Even in our flat, Mum had a little cross on the wall and she would always reference God at some stage during the day.

The commitment to religion would later have an impact on delaying my decision to tell my mum that I was gay; it was not really deemed to be acceptable in that environment.

I remember sitting in church on a Sunday morning and being made aware that being gay was a sin, or 'certain things' were sins and I remember thinking: 'I disagree with this. I'm not a sinner.'

Such thoughts and feelings made me hesitant to talk about my sexuality with my mum. I was concerned she would perceive it as being a bad thing. Instead, I focused on just being a good Christian. I loved the church building – it was one of the biggest and grandest in the area and with a celestial atmosphere. We used to go to the noon service, which was always heaving with a diverse congregation – black and white. It felt like I was part of another community. I used to love dipping my finger into the holy water and making a cross on the way into church. I would sing and pray my heart out and feel very spiritual. It felt like one day a week I was at my best for religion. 'Today I'm going to be on it as a Christian,' I would tell myself. I used to always feel like it was a way of spiritually cleansing myself.

It was only when I got a bit older that I really started to listen to the words of the priest and I started to question them a bit more, but even when I started playing rugby, I still would go to church before heading off to training. I found it quite important to go just to be connected to the process of it all. Not many of my teammates were religious so I would rarely talk to them about going to church. It just wasn't the thing to do.

I went every Sunday until I was about nineteen. By then I was independent enough to say to Mum: 'No, I'm not going this Sunday.' It was then that I started to stray away from religion. As I got older, I started thinking more and more: *this isn't for me.*

****

I think it was Mum's strict approach to parenting that first encouraged my rebellious streak. I was desperate to go out and explore the world beyond the Edmonton estate. Yet Mum was worried that I'd mix with the wrong crowd and get into trouble. I can remember looking longingly out the window of our flat and seeing other children hanging out knowing that I wasn't allowed to join them.

It was friendship that would first broaden my world. My first best friend was a boy called Ryan. He was white and also from a single-parent family and he lived in a council house which was a bit further down the road.

I first met him at primary school and when I found out we lived close to each other he invited me over to his house I and met his mum, who I got on with straight away. She became the mum that I had yearned for in the sense that she would take us out, whether it was to a park or a museum. She opened up my horizons and broadened my knowledge of the world. It felt like we would go on an adventure every time I went over to their house.

My mum was fine with that as she knew who Ryan was and knew his mum, so she knew I was in a really safe environment, just a few doors away from our flat. 'You can go and see Ryan any time you want,' she told me. I felt exhilarated.

Ryan and I remained close friends until the end of primary school, at which point we went our separate ways. I went to our local comprehensive school whereas Ryan's mum wanted him to go to a grammar school far out of our borough to get a better education. We reconnected through Facebook many years later. He now lives in Dubai and has enjoyed a very successful career.

The first time I challenged Mum came later, when I was again stuck in the flat and saw two other friends playing outside. I wanted to hang out with them, but Mum said no. So I just went anyway. I knew Mum could still see me from the window so I'd be fine, but I had thrown down a gauntlet in the face of her strictness. It was the first step to being independent.

My main friend in the flat was a girl called Stella. She was mixed race and had two brothers and they were also pupils at my secondary school. She had a Nigerian background too – her dad was from Nigeria and her mum was Irish – and hanging around with her made me feel more Nigerian. She would go back to

Nigeria every couple of years to see some of her family and kept telling me that I should go too. But I didn't feel comfortable with the idea of going and my mum never pushed me to want to either.

Significantly, Stella was one year older than me and from that day on she became like my big sister at school. Everyone knew who she was and knowing that she had my back was empowering.

I don't want to give the impression that the area that I grew up in was deprived but Mum was probably aware of things that were going on that I was oblivious to in my childhood innocence.

That would change as I entered my teenage years. Perhaps yearning to be accepted by others, I started getting into fights to prove myself. It was a bit of a north London thing to prove that you were hard, to prove that you could look after yourself – if only to serve as a warning to others. It didn't matter if you were a girl or a boy. If someone started on you, it was important that they knew you'd fight back.

Having Stella as a friend certainly helped because she was tall – much taller than me – older and stronger. My friendship with her made me feel secure, but I knew I still had to fight my own battles.

It was around the same time that my schoolwork started to slip, which further tested my relationship with Mum. I think most parents want their child to do the best they can, but I suspect most children with Nigerian parents understand when I say that the pressure to succeed is at times overwhelming. She tried to impose the same strict upbringing she had experienced on me: go to school, work really hard and get good grades. That was how you were supposed to live your life. When I started to bring poor school reports home, she didn't know how to handle it.

Her response was to try to discipline me; but it only exacerbated the problem. It meant that when I got to school, I felt like I could do anything I wanted because she wasn't there. I guess I was also reacting to the fact that because she had to work so hard to earn the money to give us a good living, she simply didn't have the time to fully invest in my hobbies or school life.

Looking back now, it must have been incredibly tough on her to see how I was behaving. I'm just grateful that she never gave up on me and her unconditional love never wavered.

Rebel Maggie, who would end up getting into fights with Ian and Beatrice and bring the police to our front door, was starting to yell.

THREE

DEFYING THE ODDS

My England profile on the RFU's website used to open with the description: 'Born with a clubfoot . . .'

The start of the profile could instead have mentioned that I'd won an MBE for services to rugby union, or that I won seventy-four caps for my country, scoring twenty-eight tries. Or that I won a World Cup and helped England to win a record-breaking seven consecutive Six Nations titles.

It could also have opened with the fact that after the first of three World Cup final appearances, in 2006, I was named the International Rugby Board's (IRB) women's player of the year (it was called the Women's Sports Personality of the Year back then, but thankfully it's now been changed) alongside the legendary All Blacks captain and fellow openside flanker Richie McCaw, who won the men's award. Or that in 2010 I was named *Sunday Times* Sportswoman of the Year, topping a star-studded list that included Dame Jessica Ennis-Hill, Dame Katherine Grainger, Fran Halsall, Beth Tweddle, Emma Pooley and Amy Williams.

Then there was the fact that in 2016 I was inducted into the World Rugby's Hall of Fame, or that I was the first-ever female winner of the Pat Marshall award from the prestigious Rugby

Union Writers' Club (to be fair, the last two accolades happened after I'd retired from international rugby).

But I wasn't bothered that it focused first on my physical disability. I was born with a clubfoot. And to achieve everything that I did meant even more to me because of the physical disadvantages that I had to overcome along the way. Not many people will know that even when I was at the peak of my game – earning plaudits for my work rate and powerful tackling – I walked with a limp. Overcoming adversity was the one constant in my journey, and my greatest achievement.

Clubfoot is where a baby is born with a foot or feet that turn in and under. My right foot was completely turned in when I was born. Mum had to decide almost immediately if she wanted me to undergo an operation to correct it with the knowledge that it wasn't without risk and would result in me spending the first years of my childhood in and out of hospital trying to straighten it out.

The operation involves loosening the Achilles tendon at the back of the ankle by taking out a chunk of muscle and then placing the foot in a cast for much of the first year. It might be a straightforward procedure but that didn't make it any less frightening for my mum.

It was only when I first attended primary school that I became aware that I wasn't quite the same as all the other children physically. I was very active and sporty as a child and my foot didn't bother me until I started to take part in organised sports like netball, gymnastics and athletics. I became quite conscious of the fact that when I ran my limp became more pronounced, especially when sprinting.

Yet although it is officially defined as a disability, I never saw it as such. I might have opted to play as a goalkeeper when we played football with the lads after school, but I just got on with it. For example, with netball you pivot and move a couple of steps and pass the ball, so I didn't have to run long distances. Rounders also involved running relatively short distances.

In secondary school, however, it became more obvious. I opted to play in goal at football because I didn't want to go out and run at people and my reflexes were good at stopping the ball. When we did athletics in the summer of Year 9, I would veer towards all the throwing disciplines – particularly the discus and hammer – but every now and again I'd be asked to join the relay team. I still remember taking part in my secondary school sports day and being put out to run the last leg of the 4x100 metres relay. I dreaded getting the baton and having to sprint the final 100 metres in front of the whole school. I was so conscious of my limp and my foot turning in. I didn't want to stand out for the wrong reasons.

I knew that I had to look after my body, but I guess it wasn't until I got into the England team that I realised that I needed to have a specialist training programme to suit my foot and my biomechanics because I began to be affected by injuries related to my condition.

One of the restrictions was the impact it had on my pace. I always felt I had good acceleration, and my first ten metres were fast but after that I would struggle and fade.

The problem was that I didn't have the right gait. Some people can get their legs to move in a good circular motion, with their feet flicking their bums. But my right leg wouldn't come round. It had little range of movement, so I always struggled over longer distances and fatigued very quickly because my calf muscle was smaller than normal.

I still believed that I had pace, but I just didn't have the right body structure to allow me to run as fast as I could. The condition also created injury problems on the right-hand side of my body – it would lead to a succession of hamstring tears, calf and back problems.

When I started to take my rugby more seriously, I decided to see a physio to help with my injuries. At that point it was identified that I also had flat feet, which is apparently more common in people with Afro or Caribbean backgrounds. The recommendation was to wear orthotics in my shoes but, rather than solve my problem, it would lead to more injury issues. Even though I wore them for long periods, I still struggled to get used to them and it led to a lot of hamstring problems. It was only when I saw a podiatrist who worked with a lot of top athletes many years later – when I was selected for the England squad – that he assessed that the real issue was the fact that the right side had adjusted so well during twenty years to the fact that my right foot comes in and I have flat feet that wearing orthotics was actually making the problem worse by trying to make the body readjust. I had to overcome psychological issues too.

To replace the orthotics, I started to do stretches and exercises that would focus purely on stretching my calf. We would also do things around my hamstring and try to strengthen the right-hand side of my body to balance out how dominant the left-hand side had become.

It was tough. As my rugby career started to take off, it was the first time that it really hit me that I had a disability. When you pull on rugby boots, no one ever questions what you do or how you do it, but playing alongside top athletes, I really felt different – and that feeling became even more pronounced when I realised that I was being inhibited by my unusual gait.

As much as I tried, my right leg simply wouldn't go through the normal running movement. And because my body wasn't symmetric it led to around six hamstring tears and the aforementioned calf and back issues.

To cope with the mental side of things, I always tried to be open about the fact that I had been born with a clubfoot. I also always tried to walk in a manner that minimised the limp, but that was impossible to do when I was running. I got a bit of banter at times about it, but I never took it as a personal insult, even though it inevitably made me more conscious of it.

It had its greatest impact in the final years of my career when I suffered a serious injury in my right knee. I tore my meniscus. The menisci are two C-shaped cartilages found in the knee joint. They sit in between the femur and tibia and act like shock absorbers, absorbing the impact of the upper leg on the lower leg. The meniscus stabilises the knee joint and maintains smooth movement in the knee. Because of the weakness in my hamstrings and calf it put tremendous pressure on my knee and the ligaments around the knee (the ACL, PCL, MCL and LCL) lacked stability.

Ultimately it required a serious knee operation, and a highly respected Harley Street surgeon called Andy Williams, known for treating top professional athletes in football, rugby and cricket, did a brilliant job at getting me playing again just in time for the World Cup in Paris in 2014. But it was touch and go. I was out for a total of twenty months before I made my international return.

It wasn't until I retired from rugby and I was told that I could have become a Paralympian athlete because of my disability that the seriousness of it hit me. I never really appreciated it at the time but now that I've stopped playing the sport I cannot believe that I managed to get through my career and reach the heights that I did and play the game the way I did with a foot that made me limp. But I did it. Another well-known athlete I'm aware of who also had this childhood condition was former England footballer Steven Gerrard, who also went on to have an illustrious career. So it can be done.

These days CrossFit is where my focus lies and I still suffer from calf fatigue, knee and back pain. But I continue to march on despite my limitations.

Nowadays when I deliver keynote talks to corporate businesses and educational establishments, I always emphasise my triumph over adversity. One of the motivations for writing this book is to inspire others to overcome any hurdles they may face to reach their potential and successfully cope with changes and the ups and downs that occur in all our lives. It's the reason why I'm an ambassador for Steps Charity Worldwide, the charity that helps people affected by childhood lower limb conditions. It aims to value and support individuals, families and careers and raise awareness of conditions like clubfoot.

The accolades that followed during my rugby career made me proud. Mum too. But my greatest triumph? Ensuring that the clubfoot I was born with wouldn't stop me.

FOUR

THE CRUSADING SARACEN

I surprised myself by listening to the advice to try out rugby. It was a last resort. I knew my life was heading in the wrong direction but before my moment of clarity after the fight with Beatrice, I'd cared little about anything and lacked motivation.

Sometimes I wonder what would have happened to my life if I hadn't jumped on the bus up to Bramley Road and the wonderfully ramshackle Saracens' ground. Sometimes, it doesn't bear thinking about.

Rugby wasn't a sport I knew much about. Like most kids growing up in north London I fell in love with football and in my area it was either Tottenham Hotspur or Arsenal. We lived quite close to the Spurs stadium so most of the kids supported them, but I guess it was the rebel in me that decided to support Arsenal instead. I'm still an Arsenal fan now.

All the boys at my school played football; at break time the footballs would come out and there'd always be a big game in the playground. None of the other girls would play but the boys would always let me. I was quite a strong character and despite my limp I was pretty good, particularly as a keeper. I was always accepted by the boys. I almost felt like one of the lads.

When I started saving goals, I'd always get picked and it was one of the reasons that I became quite popular at school. I became accepted through my sports. At one stage I joined Enfield Ladies Football Club as a goalkeeper but at the higher level I realised that while I liked football, I didn't love it. The fun that I had playing at school wasn't there.

Rugby wasn't available as part of our school's extra-curricular activities for girls. I gave hockey a go but being a goalkeeper in field hockey wasn't as much fun for me. I rarely touched the ball and when I was head to toe in thick protective padding, wearing a helmet and holding a hockey stick, I could barely move.

Netball was more engaging but what I hated about it at school was it was seen to be a 'girls' sport. I just wanted a sport where I could prove myself to be a good athlete and where gender didn't matter. Still, I gave it a go and I was a reasonable goal defence. But I struggled with the restrictions of the game in that position – such as only being allowed to play in the bottom two-thirds of the court and the goal circle. I felt like I was being pigeonholed into a small box without any freedom. It just wasn't the sport for me.

I started to spend a lot of time in the gym and when it came to the athletics season it was in the throwing events that I discovered my strength, which I think must have inherited mostly from my father. Mum said she was active when she was young and played some netball, but she's a little bit shorter than me, so I think I got my muscular strength from my dad.

I threw the discus, shot putt and I got into throwing javelin as well and was soon representing the school at the Enfield Games, at which all the schools in our borough would compete at the Queen Elizabeth Athletics Stadium. Representing Salisbury School, I managed to win a gold medal with my third discus throw (the first two were no-throws – I stepped out the front of the throwing circle when you're supposed to step out the back) and set a record that I think still stands to this day. I was only thirteen but it was then that I started to realise that I had athletic ability, power as well as strength.

Other people seemed to have seen my athletic potential too. I was awarded a £500 grant from SportsAid, the charity that supports talented young athletes to achieve their ambitions in sport and life, to buy sports-specific kit and equipment for discus throwing. But my heart wasn't really in it.

Miss Burgess sensed my pent-up frustrations and it was clear she thought that rugby would be the antidote.

'Maggie, you're strong. I think this is the sport for you,' she said. 'You have so many things going for you, I think you can be really good at rugby.'

I can't emphasise enough how much of an impact this support had on my decision to swiftly change lanes and take my life in a completely different direction, leaving Maggie the 'rebel' behind.

The intervention by Miss Burgess, or 'Bird' as I later came to know her – it was her rugby nickname – was perhaps so impactful because she'd focused on my individual strengths rather than my weaknesses. Up to that point I'd have people say that I was a troublesome kid who wasn't going to be successful.

Bird saw my strengths instead and empowered me to make the most of my talent. I think it was that praise which was the reason why she became the first teacher I actually listened to. And so, with the directions of how to walk to Saracens after getting off the bus, and an introduction to Katie, who was the junior women's coach, off I went.

****

Bird was right. Rugby would be my antidote. The game had everything I wanted, and it satiated my rebellious streak. Boys and girls played it; I wasn't judged for making physical contact with the opposition – instead it was encouraged. I just loved the freedom of being given permission to get the ball in my hands and run with it.

For the first time in my childhood, I felt like I finally had my independence and the ability to just be myself. I had big arms, big legs and on the rugby field I felt like I fitted in, whereas at school some students would judge me and make fun out of me. But I never let it get me down. After my first training session up at Saracens, it was love at first sight. From my first hit on the tackle pad in training, I remember thinking: 'Wow! This is the sport for me.'

Katie made sure that I got the ball in my hands early on and ran with it, and then I did some more tackling.

This is awesome, I can be aggressive and not get in trouble for it, this is what I've been looking for all my life.

I'd finally found a sport where I could express myself and where I wasn't judged by anyone. I may have been one of a few black players in the team – as I was for most of my career – but the team was made up of players from all walks of life and different backgrounds. That's what I love about sport. It's a leveller. Let your ability do the talking, not your background.

Mother was confused at first. 'Where has this sport come from, Maggie?' she asked one night, bewildered by my new-found enthusiasm for rugby. It was so alien to her, coming from a country where football is the only sporting language people know. But she gets it now. Actually, she's a huge fan of the sport and regularly calls to discuss the performance of the England men's and women's teams.

After the summer holidays, I spent the grant money not on athletics equipment but instead bought two pairs of rugby boots, a couple of pairs of shorts, a couple of rugby tops and a rugby ball.

'Miss, I had a great summer,' I told Miss Burgess when she

asked how I had got on since the end of last term. 'I've decided I am going to play rugby!'

'Er . . . what about athletics?' she asked.

'Well, I do like the discus, but it is nowhere near as fun as rugby,' I boomed back.

'Right okay, let's explain that to the Borough,' she replied, with a smile.

Those first couple of years in the game were exhilarating and challenging in equal measure. I knew I'd found the sport that would bring the best out of my athletic abilities but quickly came face to face with the prejudices against the women's game. The estate that I grew up in might not have been privileged in the traditional sense, but I'd loved the diversity and the sense of ambition to get on and achieve.

Women's rugby is thankfully now unrecognisable from those days, but it was a much bleaker picture when I first started out. The women's section at Saracens Amateurs RFC was situated at Bramley Road in Cockfosters, in north London. At the time it was very much a men's club with minis and colts sections. It's fair to say that the women's section was considered an inconvenience to some members, an add-on that had to be tolerated, even though we were hugely successful.

We ran two senior sides and the first team seemed to win every week and stormed the league every year. Despite this, we always got the short straw. The professional Saracens men's team trained there during the day, and then the amateur club's men sides trained on Tuesday and Thursday nights.

That meant that the only nights we could train were on Wednesdays and Fridays – hardly ideal. And that would be on the second pitch at Bramley Road, which was often in poor condition and with limited floodlights. Most of our training would take place in the right-hand bottom corner of the pitch because that's where the only floodlights were positioned.

There was nowhere really for us to get changed. Often some men were there doing some training so many of us would end up changing in the toilets. I would regularly arrive at the ground before games already changed because there were limited facilities for women. That side of it was frustrating. We felt we were paying our membership fees like everyone else and helped out behind the bar in the clubhouse – but more was put on by the club for minis than for us.

Still at least at Bramley Road we had a home. We put pictures up on the walls and showcased our trophies. When the men's team moved on to train at Old Albanians just outside St Albans and play at Vicarage Road and then at the new stadium at Barnet Copthall, which was first known as the Allianz Stadium and now the StoneX, we were left behind.

Nigel Wray, the former Saracens chairman and owner, was a great backer of making the women's game professional and the eventual move to join the men at Barnet Copthall, but I know at the time some players didn't want to go.

Bramley Road was our home and I know there was something of a protest against us moving. The amateur men's sides stayed put but there was a feeling that, if we didn't move, the women's game would be left behind. It was about respect and thankfully now the women's section is fully integrated into the professional club.

During my time as a player, early on in my rugby career, it was tough to see how the women's section was always treated differently. As well as poor facilities, we also had to fight extremely hard to get any sort of support and coaching. We were effectively second-class citizens back then and felt segregated from the rest of the club. Thankfully, attitudes have changed, and I will always be grateful for what we had at Saracens Amateurs RFC back then. And thankful to the amazing women who set the team up. At least we had a club and facilities to train at, which wasn't the case for many women or girls across the country.

****

My love of rugby would put me on the right path too. Not only did I make friends for life but the experience would also change me for the better. At school, I had lots of friends but before I found rugby I had almost as many regrets. I guess I was seen as a 'popular kid'. Even though I used to get into trouble and was often put on report by the teachers, most of them liked me too. Sometimes I'd get into trouble with my best mate, Jayne. We'd make the class laugh and misbehave, but even now I look back at those experiences fondly; it was part of growing up.

But there were also big moments that I regret and wish I'd approached differently. Getting in fights eventually opened my eyes to the fact that I wasn't acting or living my life in the best way. The fact that this enlightenment occurred just as I immersed myself in rugby fast-tracked my personal development.

So too did the love and support of others who went the extra mile to make a difference. Their actions have been my inspiration. And they included the one teacher I was genuinely scared of at school, our head of year, Ms Walker. With Ms Walker you knew that if you were kicked out of one of your classes, and she came across you wandering the corridors or hall, you would be in big trouble. But there was a caring side to her as well. She knew little about rugby but when I was fourteen I was picked to play for Great Britain's touch rugby Under-16s squad for a tour of Australia.

It was an opportunity beyond my wildest dreams but when I was told that we had to pay £2,000 to cover the costs of the tour, my heart sank. I came from a single-parent family, my mum had no money, I had no money, and I certainly didn't want to ask her for any money given her work commitments.

Yet before I had the chance to turn down the offer, up stepped Ms Walker. I don't know where I found the courage, but despite my fear of her, one morning I found myself outside the door of her office and gave it a knock.

I still don't know what made me do it, but I thought I would ask the teacher who was feared by all at the school if she could support me to go to Australia. With one look the tension evaporated. 'Maggie, I will help you,' she said. It was the first time in my life that I thought: 'Oh my god, someone who isn't my mum actually believes in me.'

But there was a catch. Ms Walker had a fundraising plan. She wasn't just going to give me the money, with no effort on my part. 'Maggie, I want you to take a bucket and go to every assembly and just tell your peers your story. Tell them what sport you're playing, what squad you've been picked for, where you want to go and what you want to achieve. Take the bucket to every class and try to collect money during break and lunch times as well.

'If you do this, I promise that whatever you raise, I'll double it.'

I couldn't believe what I was hearing. *Why would she do this for me?* Salisbury School was not a place for the faint of heart. I still remember being quite scared of going up to the older pupils and asking them to contribute to my fundraising. But I managed to speak at every assembly and ended up raising £500.

Ms Walker, true to her word, donated double the total I raised and then got the other teachers to do some sponsored events and I ended up getting the £2,000 to go to Australia.

It was a life-changing lesson in empowerment. She helped give me the tools to succeed and step out of my comfort zone. She taught me the lesson that anyone can make something of their life and own their own direction if they surround themselves with the right people, who believe in them. And, perhaps most importantly of all, don't be afraid to ask for help.

Indirectly I also learned how to speak in front of people and the communication skills that would later support my move into broadcasting.

Liza Burgess had been the one to introduce me to rugby and now Ms Walker, despite having no interest in the sport, had backed me to make something of my life. The teacher who I feared at school had become like a second mum. I owe her a lot.

The tour was seminal for me. When I came back from Australia, I set myself two specific goals – to represent England and make sure that people knew my name. First though, I had to work out who I was.

FIVE

FINDING MAGGIE

Want to know what it is like to be mistaken for Serena Williams? On the face of it, I guess I should have been flattered when I was stopped by two strangers on the streets of Moscow and asked to pose for a photograph. But I could not have felt more uncomfortable when it became clear they thought I was the American tennis legend simply because of the colour of my skin and the fact that I was wearing sports gear.

The Russian capital was the one city in the world where I didn't want to attend a rugby tournament. It was June 2013, and I wasn't even playing; injury had prevented me from taking my place in the England squad that was competing in the Sevens Rugby World Cup.

I'd wanted to be there in spite of my injury to support the team as a good England teammate. Thankfully my absence didn't prevent us from winning the tournament. But if that made the trip worthwhile at the time, my lingering memories of those couple of days in the Russian capital were one of the few occasions where I felt I was being stared at everywhere I went because of the colour of my skin. It was the most uncomfortable I've ever felt in my life.

I've always thought rugby to be a sport that was blind to both race and gender. For most of my career with Saracens and England, I was one of a handful of black players in the side but I never experienced any form of racial abuse. It doesn't mean it didn't exist, but that was my experience.

When I did notice it, however, was when we played in countries that weren't as diverse as the United Kingdom. That was when being the only black player in a squad made me feel uncomfortable, and the Moscow trip was the lowlight. I didn't want to go at the time, and I most definitely won't go back again.

Sadly, I've become quite accustomed to doing my research before I travel to a specific country. I need to understand how diverse or welcoming the culture is to people from different backgrounds, skin colours and sexualities. There's no exact science to it, but I try and make sure I educate myself before I decide on my final destination.

Russia is a country with a lot of issues, not just of race, but it is also the one place where I felt there were a hundred eyes looking at me wherever I went.

At this stage in my international career, I was used to travelling with England, but when travelling for away matches in the Six Nations and countries like Canada and USA, I never felt uncomfortable about the colour of my skin. Even before my injury, I remember thinking for the first time what I was going to say to the England coaches about the prospect of playing in Russia.

From the moment we landed at Moscow airport I became aware of it. I'd travelled with a former teammate from Saracens. She was white, with auburn hair and blue/green eyes, and at first probably saw nothing. I'd purposely booked a hotel close to the airport because if life has taught me anything, it's that the most diverse places in a country are near airports due to the tourism. But even as I walked through the airport to the taxi, I felt like everyone was staring at me.

The hotel was my sanctuary. There were lots of international people staying there. It might sound silly, but whenever I'm visiting a country that doesn't have a diverse population, I always feel more comfortable the moment I see other people of colour.

Thankfully the hotel was quite close to the stadium where the team was playing, but my anxiety started to rise when I knew I had to venture out, fearing that hundreds of people were going to stare at me again.

The moment it really hit home was when I was stopped by the celebrity hunters. I can't be sure if it was an act of racism, but my perception was that they must have thought that a black person walking the streets of Moscow must have been famous. The guy thought I was Serena Williams. I froze, unsure of how to react. I couldn't have felt more uncomfortable. I wanted to tell him, 'Sorry, I am not her.' But then thought: *If this guy thinks I'm famous, I'll just go with it and get out of here.* I stood for the photograph and then left quickly, finding a place to eat. I couldn't wait to get back to the hotel. I wanted to tell my friend that I just wanted to get out of here, but knew I just had to get through it. She hadn't been aware of how I was feeling, and I didn't want to bring it up and make her feel uncomfortable too. Ultimately, I was just glad to get back without anything serious happening.

Georgia was the only other country where I felt aware of the colour of my skin to the same extent. Years later, when I'd retired from playing and had started doing television commentary work, I was sent to the country to cover the World Rugby Under-20s championship for World Rugby. There were black players in the South Africa squad and some other commentators of different races too, but even in the hotel I felt so uncomfortable that I'd just stay in my room and only venture out for breakfast. If I wanted to leave the hotel to explore or get some food, I'd wait until other commentators (who were mainly white) wanted to go out too. I always felt safer in numbers, even if I remained acutely aware that I was one of two black people in the group.

****

Those experiences were in stark contrast to my childhood in Edmonton. Growing up I was never aware of my identity or felt that I was black. Indeed, it wasn't until my late teens that I only properly started to become aware of who I was.

Edmonton was such a diverse community that *everyone* was different. I never thought about looking twice at anyone and had such a range of friends that I never felt my appearance was being judged either. I was just completely oblivious to racism.

I can remember one day at secondary school I had to complete a medical form and one of the boxes to tick was about identity. It was the first time it had ever crossed my mind. Scanning the options, I realised that I didn't know which one best fitted me. I'd never before identified as anyone other than a person growing up in north London who loved sport, didn't mind a fight and was more than a bit of a handful at school.

For the first time I gave it some thought. Was I African? My mum and dad were Nigerian, but I'd never connected with the country and didn't feel that I was Nigerian. In truth, I really didn't know what to tie myself to. I knew that part of me was Nigerian in a sense but also felt the other part of me was very British. So I ticked the box that described me as 'Black British'. On other forms, I'd sometimes have to tick the 'British African' box, because of by parents' background, but I never felt comfortable with that term.

The death of Stephen Lawrence was the first time it really dawned on me that people might actually dislike, hate or would even want to hurt me because of the colour of my skin.

To that point I guess I'd been in something of a bubble. Deep down I knew there was hate out there, but it didn't exist in my world so part of me just didn't acknowledge it. When the news hit of Stephen's death, it became a national story and it was the first time in school that conversations began to change.

One of the subjects I used to enjoy was religious education because we often had discussions about what was happening in the news. I remember having an open conversation with different people in our class – which had white, black, Turkish and Greek students – about race, their identity and how they felt about racism.

Looking back, it was a changing point in my life. Even now I'm hesitant about wanting to go to Nigeria because of the negative stories that tend to be reported about the country in the news. Sadly, it scares me. It stops me from wanting to visit and learn more about who I am and where my family are from. Mum has never pushed me to go but, as I've got older, I've met many Nigerian people and they keep telling me that I should go and see where Mum was brought up to really understand my roots.

I've met Nigerian taxi drivers working in London who've asked me where I'm from. When I tell them that I am from Edmonton in north London, then they ask me where I'm *really* from. It takes me a while to get to the point where they're trying to connect me to my heritage. 'Yeah, my parents are from Nigeria,' I say eventually. It's then that they feel like they can start talking to me properly.

With these cumulative experiences I've tried to understand where I fit and I think now I've probably come to terms with the fact that I'm part Nigerian, even though I've not really explored the country properly.

The complexities were illustrated to me on a trip to South Africa to do some work for a rugby charity in 2016. I went on a tour of a township and my driver was mixed race. It was the first time in my life that I felt comfortable speaking to anyone about race issues having previously bottled up my thoughts.

He made it clear that in South Africa there are four different types of race and told me how everyone fitted in the pecking order. He took me to one township that was made up of mixed-race people and he said they were pretty much at the bottom of the pecking order. Our conversation blew my mind.

Two years later when I visited Kenya to do some charity work on a short trip, I found it remarkable to be amongst a population where almost everyone was black and I found it weird to see adverts involving only black people. Being in a society where black people are in the vast majority made me view life differently again. I still haven't plucked up the courage to go to Nigeria, but I think at some point I'm going to have to do that just to explore my parents' roots and show my children.

****

Coming to terms with my identity was not just about race but also my sexuality. It was not until I was eighteen and started college that I first realised that I was gay. I hadn't given it much thought as a child. When I was around fourteen, I started going out with a guy called Jordan, who was half-Turkish. I don't really know what interested me in him, it just worked. We both liked Arsenal; I guess that was the connection in our relationship. I'd describe it as a great friendship with some kissing in between. Yet however fond I was of Jordan, the truth was that I didn't feel comfortable being in a relationship with a boy. But at the time, I didn't necessarily fancy women either.

It wasn't until I left the safe confines of Edmonton that I began to find answers. One of the benefits of finding rugby when I did was that the release it gave me allowed me to take a completely different path at school. I actually became a good student, much to the surprise of many of my teachers, and with a decent set of GCSE results behind me, I headed to Hertford Regional College in Ware to study for a BTEC National Diploma in outdoor pursuit recreation.

It was to pursue my dream of being an outdoor pursuit instructor after I'd dabbled with the idea of joining the army. Before my rugby career had taken off, I had a strong interest in representing my country and felt that the army offered me the best chance to do so. I even secured work experience – one week at the Royal Military Academy at Sandhurst and then another week at Chelsea Barracks. During those two weeks I learned that life as an officer wasn't for me. But as a consequence, it made me think about another career where I was mainly working outside and helping people to be successful in a different environment.

And so at the age of sixteen I headed to Ware, which felt like I was moving to the countryside even though we were only about twenty-five minutes from London on the train. I loved the course. I got my hiking, rock-climbing and canoeing qualifications, which meant I could be an instructor in those activities, and also passed a sailing course.

At the same time, I also took an A/S course in biology, and even though I enjoyed the theory, my focus was on taking a course that would result in a job.

I loved being outdoors for those two years and spent a lot of time down at the Cheshunt Outdoor Recreation Centre developing my skills as an instructor. I did work experience there during the summer and, in the moment, felt like this was what I wanted to do for a career. But, at some point reality bit: *I love this, it's brilliant fun during the summer, but I'm not sure it's the career for me.*

I decided instead that I needed to go to university and park the whole outdoor pursuit fantasy because, even though I loved it, I realised it wasn't going to pay the bills and provide the life that I wanted to live.

And yet my time in Ware would have a major impact on my life as I left behind the home comforts – and restrictions – of my life in Edmonton.

I still remember the journey. I'd walk to Edmonton Green station, which was pretty run down at the time, and hope that I could catch the overground train with a change to Ware. It felt like a long way away and, while I didn't have a lot of money, I didn't want to ask Mum to help with the costs. So I got a job at McDonald's to raise money to pay for my travel.

There was still a rebel streak in me though, and at times I seized the opportunity to bunk on to the train without paying. Sometimes the barrier at Edmonton Green station would be up and you could just walk through and jump on the train. I spent the last year pretty much getting on the train for free. On the odd occasion I got caught, I was happy to pay the fine because I reckoned I was still money up.

In my final year I was given a free bus pass because of the area that I was from, but when I wanted to get to Ware quickly, I'd still jump on the train because I knew I could get away with it. I looked young for my age too, so sometimes I bought a child's ticket. I only had a few lectures, but because I was so far from home, I was stuck there for the whole day. I spent most of my time between lectures either in the library reading or walking around Ware, a picturesque town.

There was a leisure centre where we did some of our activities as part of the course and I'd go there to train, trying to use my time wisely to improve my strength and fitness for rugby.

The biggest impact, however, was meeting other people who were gay. If rugby rescued me from my rebellious self, the move to Ware helped me discover who I really was.

It was the first time I'd been exposed to other people outside of my close-knit environment at home. People like me. They were so liberal, not living with their families and doing their own thing. I was in awe of seeing so many people with different identities – people who had piercings, tattoos, who were happy to say if they were gay or straight. I couldn't believe how comfortable they were in speaking about themselves.

Coming to Ware, a relatively rural location outside of the city and out of my community, allowed me to really consider who I was and be more liberal not just in my views on others, but also myself. And I started to see myself change, even if it was a shock when I returned home and for a while kept my new thoughts to myself. I was gaining confidence about being different and being me. I'd spent too long trying to fit in and be like everyone else.

I didn't have a proper relationship during my time there, but it's where I had my first kiss with a girl after some friends asked me to a gay nightclub on a Friday night. I don't remember her name, but she asked me what job I did. I was eighteen and told her I was a bouncer. It was the first thing that came into my head. I just thought it was a really cool job and made me look really hard.

'Yeah, I work at this night club in central London,' I shouted above the music. It seemed to do the trick. It was a fleeting moment and, while it didn't turn into anything more serious, it made me realise that I felt more comfortable talking and being open with girls.

****

It was a feeling that would develop when I left college to take a degree in sports and exercise science at De Montford University's campus in Bedford, which has since been taken over as part of the University of Bedfordshire. At that point, I wondered about becoming a teacher, but my rugby career was also starting to take off.

I'd already been to Loughborough University several times for national academy training camps, but I remember thinking that it was so big and everyone there seemed to be an Olympic athlete. What I loved about the Bedford campus on Polhill Avenue was the intimacy of it. It didn't even look like a university; it was basically a bunch of houses grouped together. I wanted the feeling of being a big fish in a small pond, rather than the opposite. A lot of my Saracens teammates had gone to Bedford and I hoped it would be a great place to make new friends.

It turned out to be the perfect environment for me. Bedford was a nice small town with a stunning river running through it, and I could go and watch the local men's rugby team, Bedford Blues, when I wasn't playing.

It was at university that my first real relationship with a woman developed. She was called Yasmin. It had taken me some time to get comfortable with being openly gay, but living away from home made that easier for me and also helped to hold down a relationship.

I remember being invited to go to a gay club in central London and feeling completely at ease for the first time. I started to feel like I was part of a different community. Finally, I was being totally honest with myself. But now I had to be honest with my mum too.

I did not want it to be a problem between us but deep down I was concerned that because of her very strict African background and religious beliefs she might not find me being openly gay as acceptable.

My gut feeling was right. She wasn't happy, and I didn't know how to handle it.

'I don't understand, I'm still your daughter, nothing has actually changed,' I pleaded with her.

But she got really angry and said how disappointed she was in me. I couldn't accept her response and we stopped speaking to each other, which was very odd because we were our own family. I was still living at home when I wasn't at university but, for a while, I lost the connection with her.

Yet I think her first response was a mixture of shock and disappointment – in part because I hadn't told her sooner. I've since spoken to a lot of friends who have come out (a term I'm not overly a fan of, but I guess best describes the moment) to their parents and experienced a similar response.

Her attitude eventually changed from anger to reflection. *Why did you leave it so long to tell me? Maybe we could have worked through it together?*

Time was the healer. We began speaking again and started to break down the barriers between us. She explained about the values she had been brought up with, and I said that she should accept me no matter what my sexuality. It was a turning point for both of us. Now Mum has no issues with me being gay at all and we have thankfully got a strong relationship again. But going through that turmoil made me at peace with who I was. I'm completely open now about who I am. I'm just living my life, being the person I want to be, which I know isn't an option for everyone in the world.

SIX

FALLING FROM THE TOP OF THE WORLD

Life on the rugby pitch was so much simpler. I could run hard with the ball in my hand or smash into tackles without any doubt about my identity. I definitely knew who I was when I was among my teammates. If I was unsure if I had the ability to go right to the top at this stage, it mattered little. I was young, confident and enjoying my sport.

My carefree attitude conversely accelerated my development. By eighteen, I'd been called into the England Academy, which was coached by Gary Street, an inspirational leader who would go on to become the head coach of the senior England Women's team and a major influence in my playing career.

The academy was a great set-up to be part of. It was there that I first came to play alongside future England players like Catherine Spencer, who would go on to captain the senior team. My position in those formative years was in the midfield, either inside- or outside-centre, where it was felt that my strength would be best utilised. I loved watching international rugby on television and focused non-stop on three players – Brian O'Driscoll, Will Greenwood and Mike Tindall – in my attempt to learn how to play in the midfield.

My early feedback from Gary was prophetic. 'Maggie is physical and direct, but she needs to work on her distribution and handling.' But if I was a seven trapped in the shirt of a centre, I didn't know it yet. And it didn't seem to hamper my progress.

My big break came during my time at Hertford Regional College when I was selected for my first England Academy international, against Ireland in Galway. It was a dream come true to represent my country, even in a pretty low-key setting. It was also the first time I'd get a glimpse of the future.

After the match, I spoke with my opposite number in the Ireland team. I can't remember her name, but I remember what she said.

'It was great to play against you,' she said. 'I'll see you in the future when we play for our senior team.' It was such a minor thing but it made me realise that I was on a pathway. It was in that clubhouse in Galway that night that I made a promise to myself: *My goal is to become a senior international for England.*

By then I'd made the first team at Saracens and a number of my teammates were already England players – like Maxine Edwards, who captained the team for a period, Claire Frost and Helen Clayton (known as Frosty and Rob, respectively). They were fantastic athletes with heaps of international experience.

It was a wonderful time. I was learning so much from them. It felt like my rugby curve was ever upwards. Even when I began to feel a tweak in my knee, I cared little.

It happened during a match, but as I'd never been troubled by injuries before, I didn't think twice about it. When you're young you feel invincible. Yet what happened next revealed to me just how amateur my approach was to rugby – and the support that was available to me. My reaction to my first niggle was to continue to go to the gym to train and ignore it. I remember thinking: *If I keep running my knee will get better.*

Even though I was in the Saracens team – which was one of the best sides in the country at the time – and part of the England pathway, I didn't have a physio or doctor easily available to me. Alarmingly, my injury got worse and worse until one day I found myself struggling to walk. *What's wrong with me?*

To make matters worse, the injury deteriorated just as I headed to Bedford to start my undergraduate degree. It couldn't have happened at a worse time. All I wanted to do was socialise and meet new people, and I wanted to do that as part of their rugby club because that is how I thought I could establish my credibility. I was also desperate to take rugby seriously as part of the England Academy.

I eventually made contact with a physio who was working with the boys' England Under-20s squad and had a physio clinic in Bedford. He was a huge help and played a major role in my recovery back to playing again. I was out of action for at least eight months. Thankfully part of that rehabilitation was over the summer months, so I didn't miss too much of the rugby season. I still don't fully know what the problem was with my knee. Without the right support around me it was difficult. I didn't require surgery, but I remember thinking: *Am I going to continue with rugby?*

The transition from age-grade rugby to university is regarded as one of the big participation drop-out points, especially for boys, where a lot of young players stop playing or disconnect from a rugby club and become lost to the game. For many girls, this is actually where many are exposed to the game for the first time and start their rugby journey. Rugby in Bedford was popular as the Bedford Blues played just down the road from us, on Goldington Road, and I'd often cycle down and sit in the stands to watch them. And I must admit that despite being awarded a sports grant from De Montfort University – which covered my expenses to enable me to go to training, games and associated costs – there were moments during those eight months when those thoughts began to enter my mind too, with the temptation to prioritise my social life over rugby.

There were other factors at play. I'd just left home and was contemplating what I wanted to do with my life and what career to pursue. Could I make a career out of playing rugby? With so many decisions and uncertainty, the one benefit of the injury was that it gave me time for reflection – and to find some clarity. I look back now and realise that the injury came at exactly the right time for me. I didn't end up playing rugby for the university. I worried about re-aggravating the injury again and opted instead to dedicate my time to England and Saracens.

What my sports grant gave me was the freedom to keep playing for Saracens as well as focus on my professional career after uni. By that time, I'd made my mind up that the idea of becoming an outdoor pursuit instructor was not for me.

Studying for a sport and exercise degree instead, as my recovery continued, I knew that whatever I did next, I wanted to totally commit to rugby. It was a decision I wouldn't regret, and I was about to find out why.

****

My form for Saracens on my return was such that I was soon rewarded with a call-up to the England A squad. But then the call came that would change everything. It was May 2003. Later in the year Sir Clive Woodward's men's side would go on to be crowned world champions in Sydney. I'd been expecting to be picked for the A team's tour to South Africa. But when I took the call from Geoff Richards, Woodward's equivalent with the England women's side, I suddenly felt on top of the world.

'Maggie, you've been selected for the England tour of Canada,' he said. And before I had time to realise the implications of this sentence, he was gone. It hadn't yet been six years since Miss

Burgess urged me to try out rugby to save me from myself and now, at the age of 19, I was about to represent my country.

The men's A team (known as the Saxons at the time) was also travelling to North America for what was the inaugural Churchill Cup tournament, involving Canada, USA and England in Vancouver, while we were taking part in a women's event involving the same teams.

I can remember a sense of exhilaration seeing some of the names in the men's team – guys like Mark Cueto, Henry Paul, Andrew Sheridan and Phil Greening. If we felt like the junior partners, we would both play in front of sparse crowds at Vancouver's Thunderbird Stadium.

I was a non-playing reserve for our opening match but was then selected to start at inside-centre against the USA. I could barely contain my excitement. Pulling on the jersey for the first time, I looked down with pride at the red tulip across my chest. In those days the red rose emblem was reserved for the men. We weren't deemed worthy enough to wear the country's national flower. But that did nothing to diminish the moment.

The game itself passed in a blur but I marked my first cap by scoring a try. There was a bit of chat about me at the time. I'd made an impact against a very experienced USA centre, Patty Jervey. She was a World Cup winner at the time and would later go on to be inducted into the World Rugby Hall of Fame in 2014. And I knew she must have been thinking, *Who was this nineteen-year-old England centre?* I was buzzing. Yet the high I felt wouldn't last. I didn't play in the last game and a fresh injury would disrupt my training on my return to England. The next time Geoff rang me, at the start of the next season, it would be one of the toughest and most heartbreaking phone calls that I'd receive as a player.

When I saw Geoff's number flash on my Nokia phone as I walked out of an early morning lecture, I can remember feeling a surge of excitement. Then he hit me with the news.

'Maggie, sadly you have not been selected into the England squad and you'll not be involved in the autumn games,' he said.

'Ah, okay,' I replied. I didn't know what else to say. I hadn't expected to be dropped. What I really wanted to say was, '*What? Are you kidding me? I'm dropped?*'

My form hadn't been good in the first few weeks of the season. I knew that. News of the death of my half-brother Azeez in Nigeria had also rocked me emotionally. But having sampled the highs of international sport, I wasn't ready for the lows. From the high point of the summer, this was my first bitter experience of the cruel twists of elite sport. It would be another year before I'd play for England again. Like a typical Australian, Geoff gave it to me straight.

'Maggie, you play inside-centre, but you don't have good distribution skills. You need to work on your passing if you want to be a world-class international inside-centre.' Then he added, 'There are players who are playing better than you who are doing really well in that position.' *Ouch*.

After what was another short conversation with Geoff, I remember feeling completely isolated and alone. My university friends had little interest in rugby. They could not understand how low I was feeling. It felt like there was no one I could talk to. Mum, I know, would offer some words of comfort. But my England teammates felt far, far away.

I went to the gym, attempting to seek solace by training. But I no longer felt that I was a quality athlete. In fact, I started to doubt if I was any good at anything. I just couldn't get my head around the decision, and I didn't know where to start to try to understand failure. Up until that point, my rugby career had followed a meteoric rise. Now, as the students around me appeared to be getting on with the day without a care in the world, I was encumbered by a sense of gloom.

It doesn't matter how young or how old you are, whatever

level you're at in terms of your career, phone calls like that can break you. On that day I felt broken.

What I couldn't know then was that in a few hours I'd receive another call that would ultimately change the entire course of my rugby career.

****

It was as if Gary Street could sense my grief. 'Maggie, it's Gary here,' he said as I pressed the green answer button on my phone. I didn't know what to think. But I guess I feared the worst.

'I am so sorry about your news, but I would love you to come back to play for the academy,' he added.

I can't tell you the impact it had on me. I didn't care what team Gary wanted me to play for. By taking the time to call me when it would have been easier not to, I suddenly felt *relevant* again. I was no longer left on the shelf. The academy set-up was full of players who had aspirations to play for England. I guess a lot of players would have seen it as a backward step and might have turned down the opportunity to go back to the level that was seen as preparation to get to the top. But I was just so happy to be involved in a representative set-up again.

I'd spend the next year trying to solve this problem of how to become an England player again. I challenged every part of my game and my training.

Looking back, I owe a lot to that experience because, every time I have to face a setback or failure, I have a protocol to go through. People talk about stages of grief, well there are also stages of failure – accepting it, understanding what you need to do to move forward and learning who is going to support you in that process.

I quickly learned that Gary was going to be my rock, providing the support that I need to rediscover myself and my game.

When people ask me about the highlights of my career, what happened next comes close to rivalling the red-letter moments, such as winning the World Cup. Gary made me captain of the academy team for a game against the equivalent USA side. The senior men's team at the time were stealing all the headlines as Martin Johnson's side made history by winning the World Cup in Australia. Meanwhile, my road to redemption took place 10,500 miles away from the glitz and drama of the World Cup final in Sydney at Loughborough University. There was no one watching, but I loved every second of it. The pressure was off, I was playing inside-centre and I was relishing the freedom to express myself again. I even managed to kick a conversion (and I was *not* a goalkicker!). It was a performance that kick-started a year of transformation for me after Gary had given my career a lifeline. The biggest change, however, was yet to come.

SEVEN

SEVEN HEAVEN

The dossier was so thick that it looked like a university dissertation. It might as well have been. My degree may have been in sport and exercise science, but I was about to embark on a second unofficial course – a Masters in the art of playing openside flanker.

It would be a journey into the unknown. The truth is, I might have had one England cap to my name, but I knew next to nothing about forward play, never mind the intricacies of the back row. What I did know is that had to change if I was to have any hopes of winning a second England cap.

The critical juncture came as I was still coming to terms with being dropped. If it felt like my rugby world had ended, I didn't have the confidence at the time to ask why. Instead, negative thoughts and doubts swirled around my mind: *What if that was it? What if that had been my one shot?* All I could think was that there was a conveyor belt of good young players coming through behind me, who were ready to step up. Without much support at university, it began to feel like I was out of control.

I'm sure my attitude frustrated Mum. She has always urged me to confront disappointment with positive actions. 'Go and ask the question, Maggie,' she would say. But when I look back now, I just accepted it. The England head coach had made his decision: *What did it matter what I thought?*

To relieve the negative thoughts, I focused on my education. Maybe it was time to move on and invest my time and efforts into something else. After all, Mum had always talked about the importance of having a plan B. And I guess I could have walked away from the game . . . but I was driven on by instinct. Maybe it was my rebel yell returning. I couldn't stand the thought of being a one-cap wonder. And I loved rugby too much to pack it all in. To this end, I'm not sure Gary Street will ever know how much his call to invite me back into the academy really meant to me. No one should ever be defined by one cap. He knew that, and he knew when to reach out when the pang of disappointment would be overwhelming me.

What I needed was a new strategy. And, rather surprisingly, it would come from another chat with Geoff Richards. He may have shattered my international dreams by dropping me from the national squad but during my year in the wilderness he and the England Women's forward coach, Graham Smith, offered me a lifeline.

'Maggie, we think your future lies in the forwards,' he said. 'We'd like you to learn how to play seven. We think you're a good centre, but you can become an even better flanker. You like to get involved in contact, but you don't have good enough hands to play in the midfield.'

At first, I didn't know what to think. I'd spent all my years in the game playing at centre and watching and learning from the greats in the men's game on television. 'Time to go and learn a new trade,' Graham added.

They'd identified that my strengths were best suited to the back row at a time when their positional talent depth chart revealed a shortage of international-class openside flankers.

The problem was that at my club Saracens, there already was an international-class seven, Helen Clayton. And she wasn't just international class, she was an England legend. Her playing career would span four World Cups and eighty-eight caps. She was also a good friend and someone I respected highly. Deep down I knew this positional move wasn't going to be easy or comfortable. I knew it would test our friendship. She was hardly going to let me, a rookie forward looking to displace her from the national side, just take her place at Saracens. She was also one of the most respected players on the world stage and the England vice-captain. I didn't know where to start. But I knew I was prepared to do anything I could to get back in the England team.

****

It was Danny Wilson, who was involved in the England Academy at the time before he went on to coach the men's teams at Cardiff Blues and Glasgow Warriors and was also part of the Scotland set-up during the 2019 World Cup, who came to my rescue.

'Maggie, I'll help you become a seven,' he said. 'The first thing you need to do is watch the best sevens in the world. Don't watch the games, you watch what they do and where they run.'

So I signed up to a Sky Sports subscription and spent my Saturday mornings watching Super Rugby in the southern hemisphere, and my go-to players were Richie McCaw, Phil Waugh and George Smith. I also watched videos of Neil Back. It made for informative viewing. What I noticed was that the cameras didn't follow them, and they were rarely in shot. Instead, you'd only see them when they only hit one out of two, or one out of three breakdowns. It was a lesson in efficient running. In my early days of attempting to converst to flanker, I tried to be at every breakdown. Watching these world-class players, I picked up their 'cheat lines' of running. They didn't just follow the ball across the backline, they would cut across the field, anticipating where the breakdown would form, and join up with the play there.

Next came the dossier. Up to that point, my limited understanding of the role of the seven was to simply smash the opposition fly-half and cause as much mayhem as possible. Then Dan handed me pages and pages of A4 paper with in-depth details on how to play openside flanker. My rugby world was about to turn on its head in what would prove to be an apprenticeship for life where Dan delivered the theory and Graham the practical side.

First, I had to rediscover my mojo. I devoured Dan's dossier, spending nights reading through the pages, again and again. It would take a full year to make the transition, and during that time I still played some of my games at inside-centre because at that time in amateur rugby you could get away with playing different positions. It also had the benefit of improving my distribution skills. Graham would work with me outside of the England camps, down at Bramley Road, where he gave me a crash course in being a forward. We did scrummaging, breakdowns, lineouts and tackling – all from the perspective of an openside flanker. I loved the sessions (well, except the scrummaging!). Finally, I felt like I'd found my niche, my fit.

Geoff and Graham also spoke with my coaches at Saracens, so my club understood my new ambition and tried their best to accommodate my switch to the back row. I was told that I could play the first half of games at twelve and then switch to six for the second half, playing alongside Helen.

I could understand that there was no way they were going to drop Helen. She was our Lionel Messi and no team is going to drop a player like that. It put me in a slightly difficult position, though. I would be like Marcus Smith coming into the England camp and telling Owen Farrell that he would like to play fly-half, and then asking how best to go about it.

But Helen was great with me. She became my mentor. It must have been tough for her to devote time to developing a player who she knew might challenge for her place in both the Saracens and England teams. It was her competitive instinct that made her such a brilliant player. In that regard, I saw her as a critical friend. She would support me, but also challenge me – and let me know that I was not going to have it all my own way or get things easy. She was around ten years my senior and starting to come to the end of her career, so she saw it as part of her legacy to ensure that the next generation coming through were up to the task. And I owe a lot to her for preparing me for the job. The message to me was clear: *I am the No. 7 here. If you want it, you are going to have to come and get it.*

In the end I actually spent more time playing alongside her in the back row than in the centre and it gave me a close-up understanding of the role. I'd watch her running lines and how she contested for the ball at breakdowns. Then, when I got the opportunity to play at seven, I developed my own style, fine-tuning my game to bring the best out of my ability.

It took time. I made mistakes, plenty of them. At centre, I was used to waiting for the ball to come to me, and at times coaches would shout at me if I was standing out the back, rather than going after the ball. I had to learn balance – when to contest, when to support outside a back or when to step into the line to offer myself as the first receiver.

I started to love it. It was the chaos and freedom of it all that suited my personality. Flanker is one of the few positions in a rugby team where there is effectively no game plan. Every other position has a definitive role, but at six and seven it's more of a case of 'just do what you want to do'. If it's a fast game, I'd hang out in the backs and run those short lines off the inside or outside shoulder of the centres. If it was a slow, turgid game, a real battle of attrition, then I'd stick with the forwards and do the dirty work. Overall, there was little structure to it, apart from the odd instruction to: 'Go get their fly-half.' Sixes and sevens are more or less left to their own devices and told to go with the flow and read the game. In some matches you need to be in at the breakdown more often, others you're not really required to go in. The best openside flankers have the ability to constantly assess the challenges of the opposition and adapt their play in real time.

And I started to realise that my calling was at seven. When I played at inside-centre, I used to love watching Scotty Gibbs, the Wales centre. He was like a pinball. Boom, boom, boom and then he'd find a gap and break through. He was a solid unit who had gas to burn as well. That was the kind of game that I enjoyed playing. Yet there were days when my instruction was to play a passing game, and that's when I'd lose interest. Really, all I wanted to do was bosh like Scotty Gibbs and try to break through the defensive line and then maybe make the pass. The game was changing too. Teams were starting to play a second distributor and kicker at inside-centre. And I wasn't a natural ball-player. No, my attributes and skills fitted openside flanker perfectly. I loved the variety of the position and the fact that I could be confrontational while learning more about distribution skills.

I still think it's a brilliant position. In today's game blindside flankers are sometimes more like an extra second-row, which is why you see so many players interchange between the two positions, but the seven has remained 'pure' in its positional sense. I just love watching the likes of Josh van der Flier playing for the Ireland men's team, Ben Earl at Saracens, Marlie Packer and Sadia Kabeya for England Women. It is a tough position, you have to be physically strong and fit, which makes longevity more challenging than other positions, and those that overcome that have to get smarter and wiser as they get older. But those days for me were well in the distance. Twelve months on from the devastation of being axed from the England squad, I was ready to go again in my new position.

A lot of elite players look back on a season that defined their career. This was that season. The year of hard work paid off. This time the phone call from Geoff was a positive one. I was back in the England squad for a two-Test series against Canada in November 2004. *Yes!*

I remember my overwhelming feeling was of sheer relief. I was back. I was not involved in the first game at Richmond, a 45–5 victory for us, but then my second cap came in the second Test at Newbury. There was barely a spectator in the ground to see the moment that I will treasure for the rest of my life. We won the game 41–3 and I felt so much more comfortable playing in my new position. I'd learned a lot about myself, and others, during the previous year.

And now I was back in the England squad, there would be no looking back this time.

EIGHT

WORLD IN MOTION

'Mate, congratulations, you've been selected to play for England at the Rugby World Cup in Canada. Just keep doing what you have been doing.' It was another wonderfully terse phone call from Geoff Richards. I told you he never minced his words.

It was the same when he called me not long after I'd won my second cap to warn me that the funding I'd been receiving from the National Lottery was going to be cut as the model was being restructured. We were still amateurs then, but I'd benefited from financial support since my school days.

The lottery money helped cover my expenses, medical support, my training and just being able to balance university life with being an elite athlete. I'd always worked too, of course. I was more than happy to graft during spare time holding down part-time jobs, like flipping burgers and working on the till at McDonald's. My mum's work ethic had set the tone. But the lottery support allowed me to focus on my training, and for someone from my background, it helped me afford kit I needed – the training boots, the shorts, the tops – to participate and feel equal with other players who had more money than me.

I'd always been careful with my finances. The lottery support was around £18,000 per year, and it felt like a lot of money to me. I wasn't a typical student that would go out drinking on a weekend, instead I would save up to pay for my train ticket to get back to London to train or play for Saracens. With the support of a student loan and a modest social life, I was able to put away quite a bit of money throughout my undergraduate course.

My thriftiness ensured I had a financial safety net when Geoff called to say the support was being cut to individuals and was instead being directed to sporting bodies.

'The funding's going, Maggie, are you going to be all right?' he asked. I heard later that he'd rung everyone. It was a testament to his character, and I really admired him for it.

'Thanks for asking,' I replied, 'but I'm going to go back to live with my mum and start a Masters degree, so I should be fine.'

In some ways it was easier for me because I had so little. I didn't have a mortgage or any dependents and my decision to move back home to Edmonton meant that I didn't have to pay any rent either. But I know for other players it was a major issue. They had to make serious life decisions, trying to balance full-time training with the need to cover the most basic costs of living. There were different levels of funding and the top, the 'A funders', would have been receiving around £37,000. That was a lot of money to suddenly lose.

What aggravated our predicament was to see that the England men's team were being ever increasingly financially rewarded as full-time professionals who were also able to exploit the commercial opportunities following their World Cup triumph in 2003. Understandably so, they'd done something many had tried but failed to achieve. Winning a World Cup is no easy feat and they deserved all the plaudits that came their way. It was just hard to watch when your financial support was being stripped down to the bare minimum.

While Sir Clive Woodward, England's World Cup-winning coach, had been able to assemble a phalanx of coaching and support staff, and the players enjoyed rigorous preparation, which including a heavy-duty tour in the southern hemisphere, the build-up to our World Cup in 2006 couldn't have been of starker contrast. But hey, I'd made the plane to Canada, even if the seat would be in economy! I was just happy to be there.

****

I guess I'd always known that tough decisions were going to lie ahead if I was to pursue my next life ambition – to play for England in a World Cup. Women's professional sport nowadays is thankfully finally stepping out of the shadows and establishing itself in its own right, but back then women's rugby was always seen as second class to the men. It infuriated me throughout my career but at the same time it drove me on to make sure I was at least able to be seen as a leader, someone who was prepared to break down barriers and smash glass ceilings for female athletes.

My sacrifice then was to put my career outside rugby on hold, by moving back into Mum's flat and extending my education by starting a Masters in sport and exercise science at Roehampton University. It was a two-year part-time course that would at least give me the time to train like an elite athlete. I'd been able to do so as an undergraduate in Bedford and now I had another two years to breathe and focus on my rugby career.

The downside was that it felt like I'd taken a backward step. I was a different person from the young kid who'd left Edmonton, first on the train to Ware and then to move up to Bedford. I'd come to terms with my identity and had my horizons broadened by meeting new people and travelling.

I felt like I'd started my life and after three years I'd hoped to move on to something new, but now I was going back. The driver was my new course, coupled with the intent to save enough money to get a car and then to be able to move out from home – and to put myself in the best position to make the World Cup squad.

Mum's reaction was fascinating. She'd not batted an eyelid when I started taking rugby seriously. I think the reason was twofold. Firstly, I know she was pleased that I was being active. It was important to her that I was keeping myself fit and doing things as she'd done throughout her life. Yet I also think that she had a lingering admiration for the fact that I was trying to make something of my life. I still remember her look of shame when the police called at our flat when I was getting into trouble as a kid. Growing up on a council estate didn't come without risks that I'd have ended up firmly on the wrong side of the tracks – or the law. I used to get into trouble but thankfully had never joined a gang. So, I think she was just pleased that I was putting all my energy and effort into doing something that was fulfilling and wholesome. The only time she became concerned was later in my career when I sustained a concussion.

It was different with my old friends. Like many people of my age, I'd moved on, most of my friends at university played rugby or were interested in it. Back at Edmonton, it had been either football or athletics. Many of my school friends would have gone to university or college nearby, because of financial restrictions or the fact that they had families to look after.

I used to do athletics with my friend Stella, who lived in the block of flats with her brothers and mum, and I remember her quizzing me about it. 'What's rugby like?' she asked. 'I can't believe you've played for England!' Other than that, most of my old friends weren't interested, beyond thinking that it was cool that I was doing well in a sport that I clearly loved. If I'd played football for England, that would have been a different story.

My inspiration during preparations for the World Cup had come from seeing the men's team become world champions three years earlier and, once I received the call from Geoff, I set myself the target of getting myself into the best condition of my life.

We had support from the English Institute of Sport (now known as the UK Sport Institute, which provides world-class science, medicine, technology and engineering services to Olympic and Paralympic athletes) and in particular their head of strength and conditioning, Raphael Brandon. He was absolutely brilliant to work with. I'd always prided myself on my fitness and, having come through the England pathway at age-grade level, where I attended talent performance camps at Loughborough University when I was eighteen years old, and was educated on nutrition and strength and conditioning, I knew how to train. One of the foundation points in Danny's 'How to play Openside' dossier was that you needed to be fit and strong. But Raphael took me to a different level. The squad trained in clusters, depending on your location. I was with the London group, which was based in Walthamstow in north-east London.

Raf was a long-distance runner so was very lean and incredibly fit. He also knew sports science inside out and had a very serious approach. I might not have been a professional player then, but it was the first time I felt like my training was professional. We'd train with Raf twice a week in the evening; one session was on the track, which was called a speed fitness session. It was brutal. Sometimes we would run for 800 metres, stop for a minute, and then go again and again. Often the training was so tough some players would be sick at the end of it. Looking back, I was probably fitter then than any time in my career, his sessions were that intense.

The second weekly session would be in the gym. Up to that point I'd only ever trained at gyms in leisure centres. But Raf took us to a 'proper' gym, a spit and sawdust place where men wore MC Hammer bottoms and thin vests. Raf didn't look like a weights man, but he gave us programmes with fantastic detail, and other work to do by ourselves.

Given that most of the squad had full-time jobs, we were only able to get together for rugby training camps at the weekends, not like the men's team, which would get together for a couple of months for intense training before tournaments.

We had around four sessions together, including one at an army barracks where we did lots of running in heavy boots and carrying weights on our backs, which was pretty hardcore. Other than that, Loughborough was the main training base and I would have to get a lift up the M1 in a car with other teammates. The emphasis seemed to be more on fitness than rugby skills but by the end of it I definitely felt ready to take on the world.

NINE

MAGGIE THE MACHINE

The days before our opening game of the 2006 World Cup were the most confident of my entire career. I was twenty-one years old with just a few caps to my name. I was in the best condition of my life, without any injury problems and, almost equally as important, free from any mental scars of defeat.

My reputation for work rate and tackling prowess had been growing, at least in England, but I'm sure I didn't yet feature on the radar of any of our major opponents, most notably New Zealand. That was all about to change.

An incident during the previous Six Nations had left an indelible mark on my mindset. Geoff Richards was running a video analysis session after one of our matches. He would run through the match, stopping it at moments he wanted to analyse. At times it would make for uncomfortable viewing for the player in the frame if you'd done something wrong. On this occasion, it was one of my back row colleagues, Georgia Stevens, who found herself in the line of fire. Georgia played blindside flanker and had made a tackle when Geoff paused the video.

'Right Georgia, you've made the tackle,' he said, with the entire squad and coaching staff in the room.

'Now let's see how long it takes for you to get off the floor and back on to your feet to be able to make another contribution. One, two, three . . .'

He started counting the seconds. He kept going. Almost a minute passed before she was back in the action.

Now, Georgia was a great athlete and teammate but rugby banter being what it is, from that moment on she became known in our changing room as the 'lazy player'. Georgia was a brilliant athlete and for the players to jokingly call her *lazy* because of one incident had a big impact on me.

If Geoff had been using her as a scapegoat to make a broader point, it worked. From that moment on I vowed that if nothing else, once I made a tackle, I'd get straight back on my feet. It was one of those moments involving other players that would shape me as a seven. It would also lead, unwittingly, to ending the tournament with a brand-new nickname of my own.

****

In my naivety, I expected we would have the same level of support, media interest and facilities as the men in our attempt to replicate their success of 2003. My misconception was in part due to the fact that I'd never been to a Women's World Cup before, even as a spectator. My expectation was that we'd be playing in big stadiums in Canada, staying in nice hotels and would be met by people holding banners at the airports. How wrong I was.

When we assembled at Heathrow airport wearing our England tracksuits, I felt strong and powerful – and special. The fact that the tournament was being hosted in Edmonton, the capital city of the Canadian province of Alberta, wasn't lost on me.

We were sponsored by Gilbert at the time and the team colours were dark blue and red. At the time, the RFUW was still officially separate from the RFU, so our jerseys were not allowed to feature the red rose emblem. The players used to joke that it was a rosebud that hadn't quite blossomed yet, a reflection on our standing within the game. Thankfully now the Red Roses are in full bloom, and everyone is seeing just how good women's rugby is.

But really it was just like going on a holiday. We sat in economy class – as I would through my entire rugby career (it wasn't until I started working as a television pundit in the men's game that I would turn left on an aeroplane) – and there was no special reception at the airport when we arrived.

And rather than be allocated separate hotels, we arrived at our accommodation to find that all twelve teams were staying in the same place, a large, nondescript hotel next to a motorway. Our rooms had balconies, but I pulled back the sliding door to discover mine was completely covered in bird poo. There were pigeons everywhere. They must have been bored too because there wasn't much to do in the area. I remember thinking to myself: *Er, this is not quite what I was imagining.*

At least one benefit of us all staying in the same place was that I got to see the other teams in the flesh for the first time. It could be a bit awkward when we arrived down to breakfast in lifts at the same time, but I liked the inclusive feeling. It made me feel part of a tournament, even if it lacked the glitz and glamour of the men's equivalent.

In contrast, ours felt like a big schools' festival. Each team quickly carved out a section in the hotel and put up flags on the wall to mark territory. We all had separate team rooms at least. You could mingle with your opponents if you wanted, and we knew a lot of the Ireland players (who were always up for a craic) because we'd played them quite frequently over the previous two seasons and many of them played their rugby over in England. But most of the time the interactions were awkward, such as when team buses would turn up at the hotel at the same time and we all had our game faces on.

No doubt some of the more experienced players had a different mindset to me, having played in previous World Cups and knew what to expect and the enormity of the challenge ahead, but I was fresh, overly confident and approached the competition without any burden of overanalysis. It's a mindset that I'd try to replicate in the final days of my career – with the help of a sports psychologist. By the end, I tried to lose all my emotions and start again. But in Edmonton, my mental state couldn't have been cleaner.

****

The competition was contested over eighteen days with four pools of three, with the winners of each pool moving into the semi-finals and then the winners, obviously, contesting the final.

The matches were played at St Albert Rugby Park and Ellerslie Rugby Park in Edmonton. The tournament wasn't yet developed enough to merit an opening ceremony (the first World Cup had been held in 1991 in Cardiff, but it hadn't been sanctioned or supported by the IRB, now known as World Rugby).

Even by 2006 our tournament had yet to be officially endorsed as a 'World Cup' by the global governing body. It also struck me that there were barely any England supporters there to watch us. Seeing those that did travel made it feel like a part of home was with us but, overall, most of the spectators tended to be the friends and family of the Canadian side, with some USA supporters dispersed within the crowd due to the locality of the tournament, and then local people from Edmonton who were intrigued by the occasion.

By then my eyes had already been opened to the fact that the tournament would be a pale reflection of the men's event in

2003 but it did little to diminish my sense of pride when I made my World Cup debut against the USA, wearing the No. 7 shirt. Helen Clayton was still in the squad for what would be her last World Cup and continued to rage against the dying of the light and pushed me all the way, but now her position was either on the blindside flank or on the bench. But she created a healthy competition by challenging me, making sure that I didn't rest on my laurels, and I loved her for that.

The first two pool stages were relatively straightforward for us, with victories over the USA (18–0) and South Africa (74–8) but the third game against France was the one that worried us. We'd lost our previous two Six Nations games against Les Bleus and this was effectively a quarter-final match against them.

We approached the game like a mini-final: *make or break, them or us.* The psychology worked and we inflicted what would ultimately be a comfortable 27–8 victory over them. What was equally significant was our reaction. We might have reached the semi-finals, but there were no celebrations. Inside I was screaming to myself: *This is amazing!*

But outwardly I had to keep my composure. No one else was getting excited. Geoff made sure our attitude was to simply move on to the next task. The reason soon became clear. Canada were our semi-final opponents and, with the benefit of home advantage, were considered a major threat. We'd played them before and a lot of their players played in England, so we knew how good they were. They also had the superstar of the women's international game at the time, their full-back Heather Moyse. She was an incredible athlete who would go on to win two gold medals competing in bobsleigh at the Winter Olympics in 2010 and 2014 and could seemingly turn her hand to any sport and excel.

The major focus of our preparation was how we were going to stop her. Except there was not going to be much I could do about it as, having played three matches in nine days, Geoff opted to start me on the bench for a rest, given that there was only a three-day turnover to the final if we made it, and also to freshen up our semi-final starting XV.

It was a fraught match. Watching from the bench was an odd experience. The replacements also effectively doubled up as our support as the only other people watching the game were the New Zealand squad, who had already reached the final.

We got in front 10–6 but were hanging on at the end. I came on with about ten minutes to go and I could sense the anxiety in the team. With Heather in their backline, we were at risk of being carved open at any moment. And when it came, in the final minute of the game, it looked like our World Cup dream had been shattered. I still see Heather as she collected the ball from deep and simply glided, as if she was on a bobsleigh, over the pitch, eluding tackle after tackle. She may have been at full tilt, but in my head it was happening in slow motion.

With one defender left she changed direction again for the corner, but just as she was about to score, Kim Shaylor, our wing who would go on to become a doctor, flew in to make a try-saving tackle. My training with Raf paid off as I was first to the breakdown to win the turnover. Game over. It was heartbreaking for Canada. They were the hosts and had this amazing full-back who had set the world game alight. And if it hadn't been for Kim's amazing tackle, they'd have gone through. Instead, we were in the final. Just. The question was, could we make our luck count?

****

The final was staged at the Commonwealth Stadium in Edmonton. It had a capacity of just over 56,000, which made it seem like an odd choice, given how small the crowd would be to watch it. It also had an athletics track around it, which made the atmosphere even more surreal for the biggest game of my life. We were never going to fill it, especially with the host nation not in the final – and in the end, we didn't even come close. There were just pockets of people around the stands. I guess it summed up where women's rugby was at that point in time.

New Zealand were the defending champions and were a side packed with big, big strong women, with a hugely experienced and talented fly-half in Anna Richards. We did our analysis and noticed that from each kick-off, they would get the ball to Richards who would fire a pass to their full-back, Amiria Rule, who seemed to be double the size of our hooker, Selena Rudge. She was such a powerful athlete and weighed around 92 kgs.

Our game plan was for me to take a central place in our defensive line and use our line speed to make sure I was up in her face and ready to make the tackle before she could generate any momentum.

Our analysis played out exactly as we expected. The ball got to her, and she began to run at me. I practically closed my eyes as I got myself into a position to smash into her. It was like two cars colliding as I stopped her in her tracks, and she knocked the ball on to give us possession. But it was such a physical hit that I actually blacked out for a few seconds and don't remember much about it. I just remember our full-back Charlotte Barras, who was also known as 'Beanie', running over to say: 'Amazing tackle Maggie, you smashed her!'

I just remember thinking: *Wow, this is going to be a long afternoon if the game is going to be this physical.*

But it set the tone for us. In New Zealand's previous games, Rule would break through, and it would almost always lead to a try from that move. But I stopped her. It was similar to my Owen Farrell moment. New Zealand knew from that moment we weren't going to take a backward step. So many teams gave the New Zealand team too much respect. They didn't play as much international rugby as we did because they didn't have the finances to travel but, frustratingly, they would then just turn up at World Cups and win them. We knew we had to assert ourselves if we were to stand any chance, and not stand in awe of the Haka and then their play.

In the end we put up a sterling effort, but simply couldn't cope with wave after wave of their attacking play. We were a forward-orientated team – I guess much like the men – and they played with a completely different structure and seemed to be able to score from their own twenty-two without too much difficulty. We could at least say that we took them right to the wire, with a late try by Helen Clayton bringing us to within three points before an injury-time try sealed a 25–17 victory for New Zealand.

My defensive efforts didn't go unnoticed, however, despite our defeat. Sky Sports, the channel I'd once subscribed to in my bid to learn how to play openside, broadcast the final live in the UK. Stuart Barnes, the former Bath and England fly-half, and Dewi Morris, the former Sale and England scrum-half, were the two commentators. I'm pretty sure they weren't in Canada but did the commentary 'off-tube' back in the studio in Isleworth.

I'm not sure how many women's games they'd have watched before our final, but I think they were struck by my tackling, and also my determination to get back on to my feet swiftly to make another tackle. And they weren't just soak tackles, but dominant tackles. I'd make a hit, get back on my feet and make another. I can't tell you what my statistics were from the final, but I made a lot of tackles. I missed a lot of tackles too, but that was because I was putting myself in position to make them, and, as I said, the New Zealand players were powerful runners.

'That Maggie Alphonsi, she is a machine,' said one of them. And so, my nickname 'Maggie the Machine' was born. It stuck.

And do you know what? I remember thinking: *I'll take that*. Not for myself but because I knew that it was a step forward for our game. If Barnes and Morris were impressed with the physicality of our game, maybe others would notice too.

****

New nickname or not, I was devastated by the defeat. In my naivety and fearlessness, I'd expected to win. The senior players had been used to New Zealand winning World Cups – this was their third title in succession. I was suddenly struck by end-of-tour blues. A lot of our squad had decided to retire at the end of another World Cup cycle and I briefly wondered if I should find another sport to progress in.

As we landed at Heathrow, I didn't know what to expect. Would there be lots of supporters waiting to welcome us home, having watched the final on TV, like they'd done for the men's team? I was deluding myself again. There was no one, apart from a few parents like Danielle 'Nolli' Waterman's mum and Michaela Staniford's mum and dad, who were always brilliant supporters of us. The parents were all standing at the arrivals with red roses, to give us a warm welcome home. I could have cried when I saw them standing there. It meant the world to us all to have their support. But to not see a big crowd there to greet us, who weren't family, it was as if the World Cup had never happened, and no one had cared.

And yet, it turned out that someone had noticed. After several days of feeling sorry for myself and wondering what the previous month had all been about, a letter arrived at the flat, informing me that I'd been nominated for the IRB's Women's Personality of the Year award. They didn't call it 'Player of the Year' award because they probably didn't think they had enough players to pick from, but that's what it was in all but name. I was stunned. I was just twenty-one and had barely any international experience to my name. And we'd lost the final. Among the other nominees was Anna Richards, the New Zealand fly-half and veteran of three World Cup-winning finals, and the French No.8 Delphine Planet. *What was I doing on the shortlist?*

The awards ceremony was to be held in Glasgow in Scotland. Unlike my flight to Canada, I was offered a first-class ticket on the train from London. I asked if I could take a guest with me. 'Yes, you can, but if you do you will have to travel standard class instead,' I was told.

No problem, I said – that was how I travelled with England and in everyday life away! I asked Catherine Spencer, my England teammate, to come as my guest. She wasn't yet England captain but had been my roommate and was one of my best friends in the squad. Neither of us were prepared for the scenes when we arrived at the hotel. There were paparazzi snapping the VIPs arriving and also some sort of protest going on nearby. The men's awards were also being announced at the same event, while some players were being inducted into the IRB's Hall of Fame.

I got into the lift, only to be joined by John Eales, the Australia captain, and bumped into John Smit, the Springbok hooker, in reception. I was star-struck and tried not to get too excited by reminding myself they were just normal people.

I didn't pay too much attention to the awards either, and it was while I was eating my dinner that I suddenly heard my name being read out. I practically spat out my food in shock. *What's going on?*

I went up to receive my award, mumbled a few words on stage and then sat back down in disbelief. Things were about to get even more incredible, however. The big award of the night was for the men's player of the year, and it went to Richie McCaw, the All Blacks openside flanker that I'd spent hours studying on television to learn my craft. I had to go back on stage to get my photograph taken together with him, the greatest No.7 in the world with the girl from a council estate in Edmonton. If I felt out of place, I was also so elated. The pain of our final defeat was still there, but this award felt special, and was recognition for my and my teammates' efforts. I wasn't quite sure what to do with myself and I went back to my room, but Catherine was ready to party and we went back out, having sneaked some small bottles of wine into her purse.

I wasn't the first England player to win the award, Shelley Rae had won it in 2001, but at least people were starting to know my name. Any thoughts of quitting the game were banished during that remarkable night in Glasgow. For now.

TEN

WE ARE NOT MEN

My commitment to rugby would quickly deepen. After completing my Masters, I was appointed as a women's development officer at Saracens Women, my first full-time job.

I was based at their ground at Bramley Road and my role involved trying to develop the women's game by attracting and bringing new players through from the schools in the London boroughs of Barnet and Enfield.

To that end, I'd visit schools and run rugby coaching sessions as part of the curriculum or as after-school clubs. I'd then later organise a festival for all the schools that I'd coached to compete in, with the hope that some of the players would go on to play for Saracens.

I also collaborated with Middlesex University, where I started working with a fantastic woman called Stella Sipple, who was the deputy head of sport. She recruited some of her sports students who worked with me to deliver the school rugby programme. She also became my mentor, as well as my friend and confidant.

'Maggie, when you go into the schools, don't just coach the pupils, but go into their assemblies and tell them how amazing women's rugby is,' she told me. 'Introduce them to the game with video clips, your actions and inspirational talks.

'None of the girls will have watched women's rugby before because it's not on TV, so you need to show them what it's all about and encourage them. When they see that, they'll want to come to your coaching sessions, and they'll love them!'

I relished the challenge of creating an empire of coaching in the area. But the sense of fulfilment of the job went beyond rugby. During the next two years my outreach would also force me to confront issues of social stigma surrounding female sport, issues I had to contend with myself, but had tried to ignore.

I wish it was different, but even with all the breakthrough moments for women's sport in recent years, one of the hardest things about being a female athlete remains the negativity you can attract about your appearance. And this is particularly true in sports that are perceived to be masculine. Even today, some people consider it wrong or unnatural for a woman to show aggression or physicality when playing a sport, and our body shapes can make us the subject of bullying or abuse, particularly on social media.

It stems from the perception in society that, as a woman, it's deemed acceptable for me to play some sports but not *all* sports. Sports like football, cricket and rugby are still perceived to be male sports. Thankfully that perception is increasingly being challenged, but it's still an issue, particularly with overtly physical sports like rugby, as it challenges the stereotype of a woman's femininity. It was certainly a massive issue when I started out that women playing what was seen as a male sport faced the problem of not wanting to become too strong because you didn't want to develop big muscles in case people judged you on your stature.

When I started playing, if a woman had developed muscles, some people would say teasingly: 'Is that a bloke?' It was tough to take. A woman with big arms or big legs or defined muscles faced negativity, while in contrast it was seen as a sign of strength for a male player. Sadly, that attitude still pervades in some sports.

One of the things that I loved about the England team that I played for is that, despite all these societal issues, we were all bloody proud of our body shapes. Our bodies were what defined us, what made us good players. Our bodies were our tools for success.

Graham Smith was really instrumental in our positive mindset. He would tell us that we needed to build our trapezius muscles to help protect our necks. And we had strength and conditioning trainers who focused on building our muscle strength and our stature.

One of my trainers, Ed Baker, was brilliant. He was a power-lifter and had the build of a rugby player. I was always in awe of him and the amount of weight he could squat, bench and deadlift. He made me truly appreciate lifting, being proud of my muscles and what my body could do. Graham would often tell us not to worry about what people might say about us having big muscles. But it wasn't easy. Social media was starting to take off then and, increasingly, we'd become aware of people's comments and attitudes towards our body shapes.

'Try to ignore it,' Graham said. 'You might see or hear misogynistic comments about looking like a bloke but, trust me, winning a World Cup will be worth far more recognition.'

The nice thing now is that young girls can see more role models and think to themselves: I can be like that too. But it was really hard during my journey with England, because we had to live through the negative experiences while making such a big commitment to our sport.

Imagine how hard it is when you feel you're trying to achieve excellence in a sport, but society is judging you for showing what is perceived to be male characteristics. We are *not* men. We are just great athletes. That's why I love it nowadays when you hear someone being described as a great rugby player, rather than a female rugby player. When I look back now it was really tough to navigate stereotypes, societal attitudes and cultural identities. Thankfully, I was blessed with the mental strength to ensure that I didn't let it bother me.

My determination was underscored by a burning desire to share this resilience with the young girls I was overseeing during my development role, first with Saracens and then later with the RFUW.

The biggest challenge was with the under-15-year-olds, who were going through changes as teenagers, and many didn't want to stand out for the 'wrong reasons'.

I'd have open and frank conversations with them – and their parents – to address any worries they had about playing rugby and expressing themselves. Most of the time it was the parents who were concerned and unwittingly pushed their concerns on to their daughters. There was a lot of angst to unpick. Many of the girls wanted to keep playing rugby but questioned whether it was the right thing to do.

Stopping would mean they could focus on their careers and not have to worry about their body shapes and being perceived as not being feminine. Seeing them wrestle with their emotions and doubts held a mirror up to my own challenges as an England player whose profile was starting to rise, even if our sport remained firmly in the shadow of the men's game. I felt sad about knowing what the girls were going through at the time and the pressures of social media but, in a way, I also drew inspiration by trying to do my best as their mentor.

Saracens used to stage a 'school of rugby' event at the University of Hertfordshire's sports grounds in Hatfield. It would bring together the county Under-15 and Under-18 male players. The RFUW wanted to mimic what the England women's team had done with the Saracens academy, so they invited some girls along to attend too. It was very different from when I was playing with the likes of Owen Farrell as I was a physically developed athlete, and they were still young men. I was confident in backing myself.

But with the girls my main task was about maintaining their confidence in playing. The boys loved me at these sessions because I didn't go easy on them like some of the other coaches might have. Being an England player, I was aspirational for a lot of them. But a lot of the girls felt the boys were judging them and making fun of them. I knew what they were going through – it was only a few years earlier that I'd taken part in county sessions on the astroturf at Hatfield – so I saw my role not to protect them but to make sure they were totally integrated into the day and did sessions with the boys.

It wasn't possible to do contact sessions in those age groups because of the difference in strength and size, but I made sure they did everything else with the boys and if there was any stick directed at them I'd quickly step in and shut it down. I felt so proud seeing the girls, and there was only a handful of them at the time, being themselves and handling everything that was being thrown at them. They didn't let their body shapes or muscles put them off playing.

Looking back, it was those girls who followed in our footsteps that would emerge into the trailblazers of today's game. It is one of the most pleasing aspects of my career to know that I was able to make a little bit of a contribution at that level when I was an England player.

ELEVEN

PORTACABIN DREAMIN'

The winds of change were blowing through the top of the women's game as we set our sights on the 2010 World Cup. On our return from Edmonton, it soon became clear that Geoff was going to step down. But not before he would bring me back down to earth following my award from World Rugby.

It had barely received any attention until we met up again as a squad at Lilleshall for a training session and he called me up in front of all the players. I'm sure Geoff meant well, but I was hugely embarrassed as he told everyone I'd won the award.

'Ladies, we have a Rugby World Cup superstar in our midst,' he said. 'For those of you who don't know, Maggie has been crowned World Rugby's women's personality of the year.' I could feel the embarrassment course through my veins. Rugby isn't a game for tall poppies. It's a sport that prides itself on teamwork and the important role each position plays in the pursuit of victory. And yet here I was being heralded for my contribution despite the fact that we hadn't won the World Cup and I was one of the youngest and least experienced players in the squad. It only added to the perception that I was a bit sure of myself. I probably was a bit overconfident in those days.

The great thing about rugby is its ability to keep your feet firmly on the ground. My teammates thankfully gave me a lot of stick. There was a lot of banter. 'Yeah, well done, Maggie, but we're going to put you back in your place,' they said. And I was more than happy for them to do so.

I look back now with a lot of pride at receiving that award. It was so special to stand on that stage with Richie McCaw and have my photograph taken with him. It was the first time in my career when my name was up in lights. At that time, it had been a goal of mine to make sure people knew my name, especially given where I'd come from in north London and my background. But the contradiction was that I also just wanted to blend in with the team and not stand out.

Keeping my head down, however, was impossible when I was asked to sit on a players' group who would form part of the recruitment process for Geoff's successor. It was an enlightened move by the RFUW. We may not have made the final decision, but we got the chance to interview the candidates and provide direct feedback. For once we had the upper hand on our male counterparts who had to put their faith in the higher powers that be at Twickenham making the right decisions with their coaching appointments without any consultation.

I was joined by Catherine Spencer along with a few other more experienced players on the panel. Both Gary Street, who had travelled to the World Cup in Edmonton as a support coach, where he trained and worked with the non-playing reserves (those were players who were not part of the official squad, but if an injury occurred they would be called in to play), and Graham Smith were among the applicants for the position. As both had played key roles in my development as an international player, it felt strange now to be able to ask them challenging questions about their future vision for England.

I was hungry for change and improvements to give us the best chance of going one better at the next World Cup. We were still behind New Zealand. This was my moment to dig deep with the candidates about what direction they wanted to take the team in.

It was Gary who was successful in the end, but Graham would still play a key role as his assistant, and I was happy. In my opinion both men were best suited to take us forward and would eventually go on to be instrumental in changing the way the England women's team would be perceived in England and the world.

Geoff had done a great job with England. His Australian manner had been direct, he was a man who said it as it was. He had created an environment and culture that was led by the senior players, who had experienced losing to New Zealand on several occasions.

At the start of a new World Cup cycle came a new influx of players, and there was a feeling that we needed to shift gears with a new approach, new energy and a different way of playing the game. Gary had coached many of the new faces when they were coming through the academy, so the transition from Geoff's tenure appeared to be seamless and it allowed us to hit the ground running.

If I'm honest, it was also a bit of a scary time. I'd come into the team as a rookie, but after just a short time we'd lost a wealth of experience. Our second row, Jenny 'TJ' Sutton, who had been the rock of our pack, decided to retire after the World Cup. Selena Rudge, another player I had looked up to and respected, also called it a day, along with our composed and unflappable captain, Jo Yapp. Also so did my mentor, inspiration and friend Helen Clayton. It felt like a changing of the guard. Suddenly the younger players like myself, who had sat at the back of meetings, now had to move to the front of the room and start answering questions and provide leadership. We had to step up. But whether we could lead from the front in the same way as those who had departed had would only be answered in the white heat of another World Cup.

****

My off-field career was in transition too. My work with Saracens led to a promotion and I was appointed to the RFUW as a club coach officer. It was my first big job. I was twenty-two years old and my starting salary was £22,000, plus a big silver Ford Focus estate as a company car and a whole load of RFUW stash. It felt like I'd really hit the big time.

The role involved developing a talent pathway for girls and women in the London and Thames Valley region, but it was effectively the whole of the South East of England. The Ford would run up a fair bit of mileage as I visited women's sections at clubs from as far as Norfolk to Buckinghamshire and down to Kent, helping support the community game and then develop pathways at both county and regional level.

For the first time in my life, I also had a place I could call my 'office'. Well, when I say office, it was a rickety portacabin in a corner of the north car park at Twickenham. It was a tangible reminder of the inequalities we faced. We were allowed within touching distance of Twickenham stadium, but not allowed to enter. We often had to step over deep puddles in the uncovered and uneven surface of the car park and when it was dry our clothes would pick up dirt and dust. I can remember looking through the window of the portacabin, looking up at the vast expanse of the gleaming stadium just yards away and thinking: *How can there not be enough room for us in there? One day our time will come.*

My tracksuit was also a daily reminder of our second-class citizenship. It was not until 2008 when we were finally allowed to wear a red rose emblem on our kit instead of a tulip. The slights to our game provided daily motivation. I at least had a foot in the door, and I was determined to ensure that the inequalities that the girls and women faced at clubs across my region were addressed. Some of the facilities that were provided at the time were simply embarrassing. It was a man's world and it often felt like the women and girls section was just being tolerated rather than encouraged. It was not only a small-minded attitude but also so short-sighted as the recent explosion of participation numbers in the women's game – at a time when adult male numbers have been contracting – has proven.

It made it all the more rewarding to see some of the young players I worked with come through the national stage. Current England international Alex Matthews was originally part of our Under-18s set-up along with Sarah Bern, Jess Breach and Zoe Harrison, fellow Red Roses who were also part of a group of players to break through on to the international stage. To make that contribution while I was still forging my own way as a young England player at times felt surreal.

And it was not without significant challenges. It required attending clubs during weeknights when I would normally have trained myself. I also played for Saracens on Sundays, but often had to travel to clubs earlier in the day for training sessions. Sometimes I had to sacrifice my training or matches because of the commitments of the job. But I made it work. That was until the day they told me my job was being made redundant.

****

The bombshell news came just before the 2010 World Cup in England. It was hardly the ideal preparation. We'd made steady progress since Gary had taken charge. Catherine Spencer had taken over the captaincy and we'd set down a huge marker ahead of the tournament by defeating our nemesis, New Zealand, 10–3 at Twickenham in November 2009 to level a two-Test series. It was the first time in eight years we'd beaten the Black Ferns, and Catherine had underpinned her leadership with a powerhouse performance on her fiftieth cap, scoring the game's only try. Despite the inclement weather, we'd attracted a record crowd of 12,500 for the game. It was the first sign of the national side beginning to gain profile and support, a momentum that would take an unstoppable turn when we hosted the World Cup the following year.

Yet there had also been the odd blip on the way. We'd won Six Nations Grand Slams in 2007 and 2008 but then suffered a shock 16–15 away defeat by Wales in the 2009 championship. Normal service appeared to have resumed with another Grand Slam title in 2010, but again it hadn't been as comfortable as we would have liked, only squeezing home 11–10 against France in the final game of the championship at Stade Rennais.

I felt my game was in good shape. With each season my experience and confidence grew in playing at openside. I was lucky to go through most of my career without sustaining many injuries, despite the physicality of my game. At the time, I put it down to wearing my scrum hat. I know it was more of a psychological crutch, but when I pulled it on I felt invincible; it made me fearless. If I came up against a back row forward who wasn't wearing one, I used to think to myself: *She's not up for this.*

But off the pitch, the news that my job was coming to an end because the roles had been part-funded by Sport England left me facing a crossroads in my career at a time when I yearned for stability to focus on my rugby. The RFUW had employed ten club coach officers, and it left us asking questions about our futures. I'd loved coaching but wondered if this was the time to try teaching or something else.

But, in my heart, I wanted to remain in the game somehow, so when four new jobs were created, I decided to throw my hat into the ring. It was tough because some of my former colleagues were also going for them and to go through an interview process in the build-up to the World Cup was a distraction I could have done without. It was a huge relief then when I heard just before the start of the tournament that I'd been appointed as divisional talent development officer for London and the South East.

And as I was now working officially for the RFU, my desk was *inside* the stadium. I can still remember my first day, walking wide-eyed through the open-plan office and seeing all the different departments associated with the men's game. We were at the back end of the office, close to Rob Andrew's office, who was the professional rugby director at the time, and the office of the England manager, Martin Johnson.

I had to pinch myself that I was finally inside the concrete walls of Twickenham stadium. It felt like a defining moment in the evolution of the women's game. We were still the RFUW but now we were inside the building. We were considered the 'women's department', which made it feel like a step closer to the integration that would eventually come in 2012. There was a small pay rise too, jumping up to £24,000 (it would eventually rise to £30,000 when full integration with the RFU took place).

I'd be overseeing three teams within my division – senior, Under-18s and Under-15s – and appoint and manage staff for each of those teams and oversee the talent pathway for the divisional teams. Now this was a role that I could really get my teeth into and make a difference, especially as I loved the managerial side of the role and developing high-performing teams. I wasn't to know it then, but the exhilaration of those early months in my new job would turn out to be the high point of my life as an RFU employee. Sadly, things wouldn't end well. But first, the prospect of winning a home World Cup was firmly in my sights.

TWELVE

BREAKING GOOD

I have not spoken about this before, but the truth is that I might never have played in the 2010 World Cup. In fact, I might never have played rugby again.

The incident occurred not long after I'd scored a try in our 52–7 victory over France at London Welsh's Old Deer Park ground in the 2009 Six Nations. I felt searing pain shoot up from my left foot. I thought little of it and I attempted to run off the injury, thinking it was just some sort of sprain.

It was only when my foot was later examined back at the team hotel by our team doctor, Stephen Lewis, who also worked for Fulham Football Club, that its seriousness became apparent.

'Maggie, I've seen this injury before with Premier League footballers,' he said in a stern manner. 'If you don't get this sorted immediately, you may never play again and it can lead to a disability in your foot.'

I couldn't believe what I was hearing. Unlike most players, I could count the number of serious injuries I'd had comfortably with one hand. It would be the same throughout my career. But in that moment, sitting in the physio room at the hotel that night, my career seemed to be hanging by a thread. 'You're going to need an operation, and quickly,' he added.

It turned out that I'd a severe Lisfranc injury – which occurs when bones in the midfoot are broken or ligaments that support it are torn. England footballers David Beckham and Wayne Rooney famously sustained this injury in the run-up to the 2002 and 2006 World Cups, respectively. It's also an injury sometimes sustained by horse riders when they fall and their foot gets caught in the stirrups. Two of my metatarsal bones had split. I was told that if I didn't act quickly new bone would grow in between the split, which would cause long-term damage and affect my ability to walk.

And so, the next day, I was sent for an MRI scan at Weybridge and a couple of days later underwent surgery to bring the two bones together by wrapping a wire around them, which was then attached to the side of my foot with a couple of 'buttons', which would slowly dissolve. I wouldn't be able to play again until the start of the next season. But at least I would be able to play again.

****

It had been a heartbreaking end to a thrilling start to the international season. Several weeks earlier it had taken a surprise turn when I was parachuted into the England Sevens squad for the Rugby World Cup Sevens in Dubai. It would also be the first time in my rugby career when I felt we were treated equally with our male counterparts. It was also the first time I would play in front of major crowds. It was an eye-opening experience on several fronts.

There had been a massive focus on sevens by the RFU in the previous year, with extra investment provided in the bid to win the tournament. They'd appointed Simon Amor, a former captain of the men's England Sevens side and regarded as a legend of the sport and an impressive athlete, as our coach. Mike Friday, who had coached England men to success in Dubai in 2004 and

2005, when Amor was captain, also joined the coaching team. While it was great to get the level of funding that was available, it was hard not to wonder why the same commitment was not being made to the fifteen-a-side set-up given our World Cup was also on the horizon.

They'd already identified a number of players from our England set-up to be part of the Sevens team when they asked me to attend a trial at Bisham Abbey sports complex in Marlow in Berkshire. Well, when I say trial, it was more like a glorified training session to see if I had the skill set and physical attributes they were looking for to adapt to the sevens game.

I must admit it wasn't a game I'd spent a lot of time on, except for a few social run-outs. I was a runner at heart but never really understood the structure and strategy of how you score tries in sevens.

When I arrived at the session I felt more comfortable meeting up with some of the players who I had cut my teeth with in the England fifteen-a-side team, experienced operators like Sue Day, who is now chief operations officer at the RFU, Jo Yapp, Claire Allan and Michaela Staniford. The main speedsters from our England set-up had been brought over into the Sevens. I also had a level of insecurity. I knew I was a good athlete, but I never considered myself to be sevens player (because they are a different beast!). But the defining moment came right at the end of the day. The final session was a series of non-contact attacking drills. Being a sevens rookie, I misunderstood the defensive structure and ended up colliding with Heather Fisher. She was a former teammate in the fifteens side and was a specimen of an athlete, powerful and quick. She was most definitely one of the strongest and fittest players in the Sevens squad. She would probably say that I got in the way, but I basically made a mistake and my instinct took over. I ended up standing my ground and making a thumping tackle. Everyone stopped for a second in reaction to the collision. It was like two rhinos colliding and locking horns. I would say it was that very moment that confirmed my selection. The two coaches must have stopped and thought: 'Wow, we've just found our two tackling machines for the Sevens side!'

That one training session must have convinced Amor and Friday that, while I wasn't going to be a player who'd score tries (or pass!), I'd be a workhorse who could form a strong partnership with Fisher. We rarely missed a tackle and ran hard lines – could these two athletes prove to be unstoppable?

****

Due to my sevens commitment, I missed most of the 2009 RBS Women's Six Nations (as it was known then), including our shock defeat by Wales at Taff's Well in Cardiff, because we were away competing in San Diego. Thankfully, I can't take the blame for that one!

Then soon after returning from the States we flew to Dubai to kick off our Rugby World Cup Sevens campaign. I had to pinch myself when I saw our accommodation – the stunning Atlantis Hotel, located on Dubai's Palm Jumeirah Island.

How on earth had the girl from a council estate in Edmonton ended up here? It was surreal. It was one of a number of moments in my life when I look back and wonder at the situations I have found myself in simply because of rugby.

In the luxurious surroundings there was a sense of equality between the men and women's teams. Both tournaments were running concurrently on some of the same pitches in front of the same crowds, and we all stayed in the same place.

The investment brought extra pressure too. The RFU had clearly prioritised this tournament as one England were expected to win – and everything was on course until we came up against

Australia in the quarter-finals. We'd flown through our pool, winning all three games with ease but just came up short against Australia, losing 17–10 as we ran out of steam chasing a try to draw level at the death. Australia were a quality team who went on to win the World Cup, but it did little to ease the pain of defeat: I was heartbroken.

I remember we all sank to our knees at the end. The coaches must have been feeling the pain too, but I had huge respect for Simon and Mike as they went around all of us to thank us for our efforts and told us how sorry they were. They understood the journey the squad had been on. It was harder for many of the others, as I'd only been part of it for such a short time. It had been such a huge focus for this squad, there had been significant investment by the RFU, we'd been a team picked to win the World Cup. And we'd failed.

At sevens tournaments, there is so little time for navel-gazing, however. My attitude in life has always been: *what's the next job?* Our next job was a semi-final match in the plate competition against Spain a few hours later. If we lost that it was completely over, so we had to pick ourselves up and go again. It was another tough game, but we managed to squeeze through to the final. Our resilience was worth it. We may only have made it to the plate final, but our reward was to play in front of a crowd of over 50,000 supporters. My career in sevens may only have been short-lived, but this was an experience that I'll never forget. The men's finals were going on the same day. The crowd was different to anything I'd seen before, with a party atmosphere throughout the day. Men and women playing as equals.

We even got to choose the song we wanted to run out on to the pitch to: Lady Gaga's 'Poker Face'. It was electric. It was probably the first time we played properly as a team too, making light work of defeating Canada 12–0 while Australia beat New Zealand in the final. The crowds applauded us off the pitch, an acknowledgement of the standard of rugby that we'd served up. It would be a long time before that feeling would return.

****

There was an inevitable feeling of crashing back down to earth again when I returned to England from the glitz and glamour of Dubai to take part in the final rounds of the Six Nations. I couldn't have known just how far I would fall as my return to the fifteen-a-side game against France at London Welsh's stadium culminated in my foot injury. The months that followed were pretty grim. Rehabilitation is a lonely game. I was one of the lucky ones. I always feel for those players whose careers fade away on the physio table, months or sometimes even years after the initial injury, without any standing ovations from supporters to celebrate their careers. I would get to play again and experience many more highs, but even I blanked out those months on the sidelines.

Fortunately, my return to the international stage would come with a bang. Gary's change of direction as England head coach included the policy of attempting to demystify the Black Ferns' reputation by exposing ourselves to playing against them more often with more regular fixtures in between World Cups.

And so, in November 2009, came two fixtures against our nemesis in London, the first at Esher Rugby Club and the second at Twickenham, another landmark for the women's game after a midweek match against the A teams. It would involve playing after the men's international against the All Blacks. We lost the first game 16–3, but the magnitude of that defeat inspired us to victory in the second Test, for what was our first victory over them in eight years. Gary's strategy appeared to have been validated. For the first time, the Black Ferns no longer felt invincible. A year out from the World Cup, that felt like a watershed moment.

As for the match itself, it was a stark reminder of our standing at home. Dubai had been a magical experience, but here, with the rain pouring down on a cold November evening, the most demoralising moment was seeing so many of the crowd that had turned up to watch the men play disappear once we ran out on to the pitch. There was no sense of a shared crowd as there had been in the World Cup Sevens finals.

I can still remember looking into the stands as we started our warm-up in the dead-ball area and seeing some male England supporters with their pints looking at us in bewilderment, wondering what on earth was going on. Sadly, some were actually mocking us. 'You don't know what you're doing!' some shouted.

To be fair, they hadn't paid to come and see us as entry was free for our game. And now that I've worked as a television pundit at Test matches at Twickenham, I can appreciate how hard it is to get away from the stadium after night matches, so it's hard to blame those fans who cut a dash after the men's game. But at the time, I just remember thinking: 'Please just give us a half. Stay for the first half and then if you don't think it is worth watching on, then fair enough. But don't write us off before we've even kicked a ball.'

Afterwards we were told that our game had been watched by a record crowd of 12,500 – but how did they know? Some people came for our game, but many others had come to see the men. What I do know is that it didn't feel like we were playing in front of a record crowd. It was a very different atmosphere from Dubai. Still, baby steps.

'We won this game because of our physicality,' said Gary at full time. 'Our defence was tremendous, and we really believed in ourselves.'

The victory over New Zealand finally brought us some coverage in the mainstream rugby media. We'd played at the headquarters of English rugby, even if it had the feeling of an event after the Lord Mayor's show.

We were back at Esher Rugby Club in Surrey for our Six Nations campaign, which would result in another Grand Slam title for England, our tenth clean sweep, and I managed to score two tries. The decisive game was once again France, where we edged a hard-fought contest 11–10 at the Stade Commandant in Bourgoin.

Winning a Grand Slam after beating New Zealand had set the tone. The squad had evolved significantly since 2006. It was a squad that was young, fearless and was largely free of the mental baggage of the previous defeats by the Black Ferns. Everything felt different. Catherine Spencer was leading superbly and Gary and Graham had brought a new level of detail to our preparation and game plan. We were ready to take on the world.

****

It had been Gary Street's idea. He'd decided to dedicate one of the walls inside our team room in our 2010 World Cup base at the Surrey Sports Park in Guildford to newspaper articles about our team. I think Gary called it our 'Media Wall'. Except for the first few days of the tournament, it is fair to say it was a lot more wall than media.

Encouragingly, there had been more media interest going into the tournament than we'd experienced during the entire campaign in 2006. Our Edmonton experience seemed to have taken place without anyone else caring much about it. Women's rugby had spent the last four years battling for greater recognition and respect. Over the course of the next two weeks, we were about to reap our rewards. By the end of the tournament, the wall would be completely covered.

Our preparation had begun months earlier and the intensity of our training was markedly different from our 2006 campaign. It might have still been light years behind what the men would do the following year before their World Cup in New Zealand, but we benefited from greater investment because we were hosting the tournament and the rewards of winning it would far outweigh the cost.

But greater expectation brought greater pressure.

In 2006 it was fair to say that we'd been perceived as a team with the potential to win, but the consensus was that New Zealand were the strong favourites. Four years later, given our victory at Twickenham, the odds seemed more balanced. We'd won five Six Nations in a row, won two Nations Cups, won the last European Cup and beaten New Zealand for the first time in eight years in the double-header challenge.

Catherine Spencer had emerged as a formidable captain and worthy successor to Jo Yapp. She was over 6ft tall and was the type of player who led from the front. But there was pressure on her, and all of us, to win. It was something we tried to embrace. Our unofficial team motto became: 'There is no life after the World Cup.' Given that within our squad we had a vet, several teachers, a few policewomen and physiotherapists, it was quite a statement. Some quit their day jobs to be fully prepared.

I couldn't wait to get stuck in. We frequently met up for weekend training camps at Loughborough and Lilleshall – as amateurs it was still not possible to ask players to take weeks off work. In total we had fifty training days together, spread over locations across the country. One of the planks of Gary's philosophy was to bring us closer together so that when the pressure came on the bonds would not break, and in his pre-tournament interviews he spoke of the differing approaches to coaching women and men.

'There are a lot of values and trust that is inherent in female team sports; they like a sense of fair play,' he said, in the build-up to the tournament. 'There's a phrase we use: whereas boys battle to bond, girls have to bond to battle. You could split up boys into a red and blue team and play a game and afterwards the boys would all be mates, they'd just go for a beer. Because you've battled, you've bonded. You wouldn't necessarily get that with girls. But now this squad has really bonded, and they'll battle to the end.'

It was not the first time he would be proved to be right.

THIRTEEN

THE TIPPING POINT

People of a certain age may remember the iconic television advert for Levi 501 jeans made famous by the late Nick Kamen in the 1980s when the former model stripped down to his boxer shorts to the soundtrack of Marvin Gaye's song 'Heard it Through the Grapevine' in a laundrette.

Well, fast forward to September 2010 and I experienced my own surreal moment in the laundrette of the Surrey Sports Park. No one was stripping down to their undies and the only soundtrack was the whirring and clanking of the machines. But as I lugged my bag of dirty kit through the door, I looked across to see Anna Richards, the veteran New Zealand fly-half, already there, sitting waiting for her washing cycle to complete. Moments later, Debby Hodgkinson, the Australia No.8, joined us. You couldn't make it up.

If you wanted a stereotypical snapshot of the difference between men's and women's elite sport, then surely this was it. I cannot imagine seeing any of Martin Johnson's England squad at the time having to lug their washing to a laundrette and sit there for a couple of hours in awkward silence with their opposite numbers during the 2011 men's World Cup in New Zealand.

Still, it was one of the aspects of the tournament that I came to love. The men didn't know what they were missing out on! Anna Richards was a legend of the game. Debby was one of the most fearsome back row opponents in the world. She was my nemesis. And yet once we got over the obvious awkwardness of the impromptu meeting, we started talking and got to know each other a little better. 'You're one of the nice ones in the England team,' Debby said to me. I don't think she was very fond of my England teammates, but thankfully she'd warmed to me.

'Thanks . . . I don't think I'm allowed to talk to the enemy.' I replied jokingly. She was a remarkable athlete, taller than me and with a surfer's appearance. She was much cooler than I was! We would say hello to each other when we bumped into each other in the World Cup village or when we went for food.

One morning I went down for breakfast and shared a table with some of the Ireland and Kazakhstan teams in the massive canteen area of the university.

We ended up building relationships and ended up as friends, even though I constantly had to give off this game-face impression that I was there to win a World Cup. We were getting to know our enemies. And getting to know the person behind the opponent made it even more special. It was just a number of enriching experiences that made the 2010 World Cup not only the tipping point for the rapid growth of women's rugby, but also my favourite of all the three tournaments I would play in.

****

I say that now, but it was a sentiment far from my mind when our preparations began a few months earlier. New Zealand remained the overwhelming favourites for the tournament but had only played six games since lifting the trophy in Edmonton four years earlier. Their lack of game time together was something that gave us hope. To take full advantage, Gary wanted us to be fitter than anyone else and that meant a major focus on strength and conditioning at various camps across the country – including an army camp in the Brecon Beacons.

It was brutal. The fitness work was extreme, but it went far beyond that, including sleep deprivation. We had to go for a yomp, then set up camp in pairs and sleep under a canopy. We would then have to keep watch on shifts during the night to look out for the 'enemy', which involved some of the army soldiers acting as enemy forces in an attempt to capture us. My partner was Catherine Spencer. The concept was to test our decision-making process under pressure, without sleep or food. It was tough for two reasons; one because I loved sleep and food, and two, you didn't want to be around Spencer when she'd been deprived of sleep. She was like an angry bear that had been woken up early from hibernation!

The next day we would have to work as teams to carry a water tank around an obstacle course, we did zip-wire exercises, bridge-building and a host of other military team-building exercises and scenarios to develop our leadership, teamwork and problem-solving skills.

Spencer and I had a laugh when we could, but we were broken. We just had to get on with it. The exercises definitely brought us closer together, but there were times when I couldn't help thinking: *How on earth is this going to help us win a rugby match? Is this the best preparation to win a World Cup?*

Sports science was advancing, including nutritional advice and video analysis. We even knew how much salt we lost after a training session. The commitment from the girls was incredible. Some, like Spencer, gave up their day jobs that summer just so they could totally devote themselves to the training. And remember, this was at a time when, unlike the England men's team, we were still amateurs, playing simply for the pride of representing our country. At the start of the year, we were given £1,000 to cover our expenses. It barely lasted through January. At the time the England men's players would have received over ten times that amount just for playing in one match.

'These girls are as passionate as any group I've ever been involved in,' said Gary in the build-up to the tournament. 'If we dictate our own destiny then we'll do really well. It's our choice.'

Despite my misgiving about the army camp, I headed into that tournament in the best shape of my life. We were ready.

I'd never felt as close to my teammates. Four years earlier I was a rookie, who was still pinching myself that I was involved. Now I felt like I was worthy of my place and was an important figure in the group. We were physically and mentally in great shape. I felt that we'd done everything we possibly could to put us in the best position to go one step further than Edmonton.

Gary even brought in Martin Johnson to address us in the final week before we kicked off. For the first time, the tournament was going to be televised by Sky Sports and, finally, the mainstream media began to show some interest. The wall, slowly but surely started to fill up. Gary was helping to fill it himself. 'We're getting more media coverage now and we want to show how well and skilfully women can play the game,' he said in an interview. 'We can go to new levels, and we want to produce a product that allows us more time, investment and input. It will be the most important couple of weeks ever in the game. It could be the tipping point.'

****

We felt the responsibility. At the time there were around 15,000 female rugby players in England, and more than half were at youth level. As tournament hosts, I desperately wanted us to put on a show that would capture the nation's attention. I knew the best way to do that was to win it.

It was still two years before the London Olympics would take interest in women's sport to a new level. The year before, the England women's cricket team had won the ICC Women's T20 World Cup but it hadn't really cut through. This was our opportunity and, encouragingly, interest would grow through the tournament.

In part that was due to the Olympic spirit that was being generated on the campus. In Edmonton we'd all been stuck in one hotel, but in Guildford we had our own accommodation blocks. Flags were hung from the windows to mark out territories and mini villages. We had our own village; Ireland and the USA did the same. It felt like a proper international tournament, and I just loved the atmosphere – a potent mix of camaraderie and national pride. It felt like we were staying in an Olympic village.

To generate press interest, the organisers staged a major pre-tournament press conference at City Hall in Southwark, on the south bank of the Thames. Spencer did a great job as host captain in talking passionately about the impact the tournament could have for women's rugby. It was a rare opportunity in this country to stand alone as a female rugby player, the England captain no less, and receive press attention without being overshadowed by our male counterparts.

The competition would run over sixteen days and involve thirty matches between twelve nations, divided into three pools of four teams. New Zealand, England and France, who had finished in third place in 2006, were given the top ranking in each of the three pools.

We stormed through the pool stages, defeating Ireland 27–0, Kazakhstan 82–0 and the USA 37–10. We were flying. All the work before the tournament seemed to have paid off.

While I was desperate to play our knockout matches in front of a big crowd, I had also loved the intimacy of the pool stages, which were all staged at the Surrey Sport Park.

Every game had a sense of ritual about it. We would dress in our kit and wear our tracksuits over the top – our 'presentation kit' – and then walk as a team around 100 metres down to the pitches that were covered in Rugby World Cup branding, our accreditation passes hanging around our necks. It would be the same for every team, even New Zealand. We would take off our tracksuits in the small changing rooms before kick-off and each pitch was decorated with the World Cup branding, and the World Cup music 'World in Union' was blaring out of some speakers. It felt like we were really in a tournament. Women's rugby was on the move.

If we'd played pretty much alone in Canada, this time we had plenty of friends and family watching at the side of the pitches.

The capacity for each game was 2,500 and every game was sold out. It was remarkable. Overlooking each pitch was the Sky Sports gantry and some of their main rugby pundits at the time – like Will Greenwood, Stuart Barnes and Dewi Morris – were so close to the action that at times we could hear their match commentary during the games.

Supporters could buy day passes which enabled them to watch all the games that day. Others opted for the cheaper view of sitting in the Starbucks on the campus, from where you could see our pitches while sipping coffee! Oh well, the atmosphere and sense of occasion felt special to me. It was a wonderful mix of an amateur and 'professional' spirit and critically it laid down a marker for future tournaments – if you wanted to host a World Cup, this was the way to do it.

The semi-finals were a different story again, staged at Harlequins' ground, The Stoop, which took the profile of the tournament to a new level. We faced Australia – including Debby and her freshly laundered kit. Going head to head with my pal from the laundrette just added to the occasion. I remembered shooting her a look before the game and forcing myself to think: 'For the next eighty minutes, I am really going to dislike you!' I couldn't drop my guard now.

We ended up winning the game quite convincingly. Spencer scored a try after just six minutes and we never looked back, with Danielle 'Nolli' Waterman scoring another try in the first half. I managed to make some breaks to keep us on the front foot and eventually a penalty by Alice Richardson two minutes from time completed a 15–0 win. Yet during the contest it felt anything but easy. The scoreline flattered us.

I think we were helped by the fact that Australia had, like many teams (we would do the same to a greater extent), made the sevens team their priority, which inevitably meant that their fifteen-a-side team suffered as a consequence. We hadn't played a Test match against them for nine years before our semi-final encounter. Touch rugby was also a major draw on playing talent in Australia. It was tough on them to ask them to come together as a fifteens squad once every four years. But they still have some superstar players, like Debby and Shannon Parry.

The two standout moments in the game didn't involve tries, however. They were moments of the kind of physicality that people at the time didn't associate with the women's game. At times, people who had never seen us play before would ask if we tackled each other with the same aggression as the men and would question if we had the same passing and kicking skills. Well, in the nineteenth minute of our semi-final, a tackle by Australia wing Nicole Beck on Fiona Pocock actually went viral. Fiona looked to be on course to score one of the tries of the tournament after we'd run the ball out of our own half, and she used her pace and side-stepping ability to round the Australian fullback Tricia Brown.

Yet, seemingly from nowhere, Beck shoots across the pitch to hit Fiona with a thumping tackle, knocking her into touch. It was a tackle that Cheslin Kolbe, the South African wing, would have been proud of. If you haven't seen it, you can still find it on YouTube. It's worth a look. Sadly, for Fiona, she hurt her knee as a result of the tackle and was ruled out of the final.

Beck got a taste of her own medicine in the second half when, as she dashed towards the line, Nolli smashed her into touch with almost an identical tackle. Anyone watching those hits would be left in no doubt about the physicality of women's rugby. If some people didn't think it was appropriate for young ladies to play in such an aggressive manner, well *tough*. We were elite athletes, playing rugby like elite athletes. Our gender didn't matter. I can remember afterwards hearing some of the supporters talking with an element of surprise. 'Those women have a bit of bad ass about them,' one said. 'Bloody hell, that was an impressive bit of rugby,' said another.

In an interview after the game, Nolli was asked about her tackle. No big deal. 'I was just doing my job as a defender to stop them from scoring,' she said. 'We take so much from the strength and conditioning drills, and Graham Smith always comes up with great new contact drills. Mind you,' she added, 'one of Maggie's hits against France was the hardest there's ever been in a women's match.' I'll take that Nolli, thank you.

I loved the game against Australia. It was one of my best in an England shirt. I carried all night and even got a few passes away – before contact – that would have brought a smile to Geoff Richards' face.

Bring on New Zealand.

Before the final, I was asked for my reflections on our meeting four years ago in Edmonton. 'I felt when we were out there that both teams were playing above what they'd done before,' I said. 'What I learnt is that there doesn't have to be limits to your game.' Our only limits now were the blue skies over south-west London.

****

Surely this was our moment. I remember the drive from our accommodation to The Stoop gave us the first real sense that public interest was growing like never before. The journey along that A316 felt like the tipping point that Gary had hoped for. The traffic was heavy, cars were parking in the Rosebine car park, which is used for Harlequins and England men's matches at Twickenham, there were even ticket touts, people were carrying red rose flags (we'd finally been allowed to wear the red rose emblem on our shirts the previous year in anticipation of the full merger of the RFU and the RFUW). At the end of a BBC news programme shown earlier in the day, the man presenting the weather forecast referenced our match, describing the expected weather conditions and they only do that if the event is of public interest and is expecting large crowds to attend, like you would expect with Wimbledon or Glastonbury. Slowly but surely our sport was finally beginning to seep into the national sporting psyche.

We were at home. The Stoop was going to be a 14,500 sell-out, almost entirely made up of England supporters. The weather was perfect. I didn't need the BBC weather forecaster to tell me the sun was going to shine on us on the afternoon of Sunday, 5 September 2010. It would be a new world record crowd, and we were being interviewed by the national press, with a number of the rugby correspondents attending the match.

Our communications manager, Julia Hutton, posted all the cuttings up on our media wall. I think the number of stories even surpassed Gary's pre-tournament hopes. In 2023, England's 'Red Roses' were watched by a world record crowd at Twickenham of over 58,000 to see the side defeat France to win another Grand Slam. I like to think that our final in 2010 was the foundation stone for that remarkable growth of interest.

I remember thinking in the build-up to the game of all the people who had helped shape my rugby career, from Liz Burgess to my Saracens coaches Katie Ball and Amanda Bennett – all had contributed to my development and the growth of the women's game in the UK.

But, when the final whistle blew, my overriding emotion was regret. New Zealand had been there for the taking. Anna Richards, their talisman, was forty-five years old. She'd been in my sights throughout the afternoon. Surely her best days were behind her.

I'd run and run all afternoon. New Zealand creaked at key moments. They had three players sent to the sin bin for killing the ball as they tried to slow down our tempo. At one stage, they were reduced to thirteen, which was our time to strike. We lost it because there weren't enough leaders to navigate the match. It was in those white-hot moments that we missed some of the veterans of the 2006 side. If the evolution over the last four years had transformed our game, we lacked the ruthless instinct of experience.

We'd spent much of the first half defending for our lives, with Nolli at her best again, another fearsome tackle on Kelly Brazier preventing what looked like a certain try while New Zealand also missed two relatively simple penalty kicks at goal – by Brazier and Emma Jensen. We started to frustrate them via our maul and the frustration appeared to boil over when they received two yellow cards, with Richards and centre Mel Bosman sent to the sin bin.

But now it was our turn to be frustrated. We forced things instead of sticking to our game plan and making the numbers count. Teams often rally when they are down to fourteen players

– but thirteen? We should have done so much better, but I felt we struggled with the pressure of knowing that we should take advantage of our numerical advantage.

Instead, it was New Zealand who took the lead when they returned to fourteen, with Carla Hohepa scoring a try, just after Brazier had kicked a penalty to the corner. When Katy Daly-Mclean missed a couple of kicks at goal before half-time, the tension only mounted. *Stick to our game plan, we have to stick to our game plan.* But the pressure was suffocating and New Zealand sensed it. There was a reason why they hadn't lost a World Cup match since 1991, when they suffered a shock semi-final defeat by the USA.

Katy cut our deficit to four points with a penalty after the restart but New Zealand, sensing the danger, again took control. Brazier was short with a penalty attempt before Hohepa broke free only to be tackled at the corner by Joanna McGilchrist, while Richards also went close.

When Brazier slotted a penalty to restore the seven-point advantage in the fifty-sixth minute, the game seemed to be slipping from our grasp. There were twists still to come, however. Surprisingly a flash of indiscipline by Melissa Ruscoe opened the door for us again. Amy Turner came close to powering over, and we opted for a series of five-metre scrums. A penalty try looked on the cards but then Catherine Spencer fed Amy Turner, and then Charlotte Barras, who had started the game in place of the unfortunate Fiona Pocock, sliced through the cover defence for an excellent try. When Katy landed a superb touchline conversion, we were level again and had an extra player advantage.

But, heartbreakingly, it wasn't to be. Brazier landed another penalty to restore their lead and with the pressure mounting again we found ourselves increasingly forced to play from deep within our half. At the final whistle, we all sunk to our knees. It had been the greatest contest in the history of women's rugby, but we'd fallen short, despite everything we had done to prepare ourselves for glory.

Even now, I look back at that missed opportunity with a mixture of anger and frustration. Sir Clive Woodward, who coached the England men's team to World Cup glory in 2003, prepared his side for what he described as 'TCUP' moments – 'thinking correctly under pressure'. It resonated with me because we just hadn't done that throughout the eighty minutes.

When we had levelled the scores at 10–10, and with an extra player, I totally backed us to go on and win the final, even if it meant taking the game to extra time. We were the fitter team, no doubt. Instead, we handed the initiative back to the Black Ferns when one of our players went off their feet at a breakdown in our twenty-two, giving Brazier the opportunity to restore their lead. It took a while to get over what happened but years later, when I would give leadership talks based on my rugby experiences, I would highlight that moment. The player who went off their feet might have given away the decisive penalty, but the game was not lost in that moment. Collectively we had lost the game over the course of the eighty minutes, for a variety of reasons. We needed to own the defeat collectively, not attach blame to any individual. Together, as one, we had lost the final. It was a lesson we would never forget, but one that would make us stronger.

FOURTEEN

'DOCTOR OF RUGBY'

In the aftermath of the tournament, I faced a tipping point of my own.

It took many days to overcome the disappointment of losing our final. It had been my target for four years. Even though it felt like we'd smashed the glass ceiling that had been holding women's rugby back, we all knew we'd squandered a golden opportunity to really thrust our sport into the public domain if we'd become world champions. The country was entering the final stages of preparing for hosting the Olympics in 2012. Imagine the feel-good factor we could have created by stealing a march on what would become known as the Golden Games?

The dichotomy facing me was that despite the pain at losing the final, my personal profile was starting to soar. It had begun even as the tournament went on and only accelerated after the final.

Just as the aftermath of the 2006 World Cup left me feeling awkward about receiving the IRB's Women's Personality of the Year award, now I started to receive accolades in the wake of our final defeat that, for the first time, would see me question whether it was time to move on from rugby. It would also lead to a series of remarkable life events, including picking balls out of a bag with Boris Johnson, sharing a cup of tea with another former Prime Minister, David Cameron, becoming an ambassador for the men's 2015 World Cup . . . and experiencing the three worst minutes of my life during the ceremony at Buckingham Palace to receive an MBE for services to rugby.

My life began to change when, the month after our final, the *Sunday Times* launched their Sportswoman of the Year award, and I was selected by the judges – chaired by BBC Radio 5 Live's Eleanor Oldroyd – on a shortlist of six. I was stunned. At the time this was one of the most prestigious awards in women's sport. Previous winners included Sally Gunnell, Dame Tanni Grey-Thompson, Denise Lewis, Dame Kelly Holmes, Rebecca Adlington and Victoria Pendleton – all household names in British sport.

The shortlist included some of *my* heroes and was star-studded. I was up against Jessica Ennis (now known as Dame Jessica Ennis-Hill) who would become the golden girl of the London Olympics and the heptathlete was already being used to promote the Games, had won gold medals at the World Indoor Championships and European Athletic Championships. Amy Williams, the skeleton rider who had won a gold medal for Team GB at the Vancouver Winter Olympics, Britain's first individual champion for thirty years, had also been shortlisted along with Fran Halsall, who had won ten medals, including three golds at the European Swimming Championships in Budapest and the Commonwealth Games in Delhi.

The final two were Emma Pooley, who had become the first British cyclist to win the Tour de L'Aude and won the Road World Championships in Melbourne; and Beth Tweddle, our most decorated gymnast, who had recently won gold on the uneven bars at the World Artistic Championships in Rotterdam – her third world title in four years.

In comparison my citation from the judges seemed a little underwhelming. 'A number of impressive performances and hard-hitting tackles at the women's rugby World Cup finals established the twenty-six-year-old England flanker as the world's leading female international player.'

I'd won nothing. I was not even the England team's captain. *Oh well*, I thought. *At least I'll get the chance to dress up and mingle with some of Britain's best athletes.*

The presentations were held at the headquarters of the British Olympic Association in London. Voting was open to the public and for that reason I didn't think for a moment that I'd win. I knew who everyone else was on the shortlist. But would they really know who I was? All I'd won was a few league titles with Saracens. It's no exaggeration to say that I travelled to the event in a state of disbelief. Negative thoughts kept flashing through my mind: *What am I doing here?* I'm not sure you could even call it imposter syndrome, as I simply couldn't compete with the success (and medals to back it up) of the others on the shortlist.

It was like a freeze-frame moment in my life when I heard my name called out as the winner. *What? Did I just hear that right?* Apparently, I'd won by an overwhelming margin. I was speechless. I couldn't get my head around it. I played in one of the ultimate team sports for a side that had just lost a World Cup final. But, against all the odds, the public had voted for me.

'To win had been a distant thought for me,' I said in an interview afterwards. 'Then to hear my name, and to hear that the poll was a record, was incredibly special. Even better, it was something decided by the public. I felt that I was the underdog, and I have to give a massive thank you to everyone who supported me.'

Stephen Jones, the legendary rugby correspondent of the *Sunday Times*, a man who has done much to support the women's game, afterwards wrote that the reason I'd won was that I had achieved something that none of the others had.

'She changed her sport forever, shifting the whole thing on its axis,' Jones wrote. 'The World Cup was an extraordinary success, and the profile of women's rugby was illustrated by a 13,000 crowd for the final, and a record global television audience.

'In all of this, a dedicated, high-quality and personable England team played a leading role. Alphonsi was the talisman, the Pied Piper. She is uncomfortable being detached from the collective for praise, but she was easily the figure of the tournament, so brilliant as a flanker, so imposing in attack and defence and so wonderful at the breakdown.

'It was one of the greatest individual performances I have seen from either sex. It was her thunderous physicality that stood out above all else. The tournament saw such a physical crunch to proceedings that all remaining reservations about the ability of women to play powerful rugby at elite level were scattered to the four winds.

'Alphonsi was explosive. There was a roar every time she was in possession. She made bursts and tackles of such power that to the uninitiated they must have seemed frightening. Rebecca Alphonsi, her mother who drove her thousands of miles in the formative sporting years, may or may not have watched it all with eyes closed. Maggie has given new impetus to the growth of the game, impressed so many doubters, changed the perception of others, and changed the way it is played forever.'

Wow. My life was about to become unrecognisable too. I wanted to remain modest but also appreciate the moment. I knew now that when I visited a rugby club, the result might be that they would start up a girls' or women's team because the chairman and committee might know who I was now. But the increasing fame would also bring temptations away from the game.

Right: Baby Maggie.

Below: Picture of me in U16 London & Home Countries Regional Team at Lichfield (I'm bottom right corner).

Edmonton Green in London where I grew up.

With two of Salisbury secondary school PE teachers: Liza Burgess is in the middle, Louise Canty is on the left.

Above: Training hard ahead of the 2014 World Cup.

Right: Playing Samoa in our change shirt at the 2014 World Cup.

Catching up with my Saracens teammates in Paris before I was late for Graham's training session.

Moving in to shut down a Canadian attack during the World Cup final.

All smiles (despite the fatigue) during our army camp in the Brecon Beacons ahead of the 2010 World Cup.

It's always special to share a moment with those who support you after a match – this time during the 2010 World Cup. In the bottom right-hand corner is a future England star, a young Hannah Botterman!

Above: In action for Saracens against Lichfield in 2014.

Left: The try I scored against France after returning back from being out for twenty months.

Right: With Mum at my graduation.

Below: Early years at Saracens, here playing in the club's 125th anniversary season in 2001.

Left: Fighting to break through a tackle against Ireland in the Six Nations.

Below: Playing against Canada in the plate final of the Rugby Sevens World Cup in Dubai in 2009.

Above: Delivering a coaching and leadership session to some young rugby stars.

Right: Chasing an Olympic dream. It may not have worked out, but I loved my time doing the shot put again.

Above: My studio debut for a men's Six Nations match, joined by presenter Mark Poutgach, Jonny Wilkinson and Sir Clive Woodward.

Right: With the Six Nations trophy as I preparing for pitch side analysis with ITV Sport.

Below: With my agent, Julia Hutton, at the ATP tennis finals at the O2.

Above: Winning Team of the Year at SPOTY.

Right: With the World Cup at 10 Downing Street.

Definitely stepping out of my comfort zone: taking part in Gareth Malone's All-Star 'Children in Need' choir.

With my MBE at Buckingham Palace.

Right: Heading up to recieve my medal wearing an England flag in style of Jessica Ennis-Hill during the 2012 Olympics.

Below: After years of heartbreak and hard work, we finally reached the promised land.

The changing room celebrations begin after the final.

Front pages of the national papers the next day. It was the first time women's rugby had ever been plastered across the front pages of most of the national newspapers. It shows the impact our win had and how after many years barely being mentioned on the back pages we finally were front and centre.

Joining my colleagues on the RFU council.

Bing inducted into the World Rugby Hall of Fame alongside some true rugby royalty.

Above: Our wedding day.

Left: Celebrating Global Clubfoot Day 2023 with Marcella and our children, Artie and Willow.

****

In January 2011, I found myself back at another prestigious awards event, this time to receive the main award at the Rugby Union Writers' Club's fiftieth annual dinner in London. Remarkably, I was chosen ahead of All Blacks flanker Richie McCaw and the South Africa lock Victor Matfield to receive the Pat Marshall Memorial Award, which had been won the previous year by Ireland and Lions legend Brian O'Driscoll. This was uncharted territory, winning awards ahead of my male counterparts, and legends of the game at that.

Suddenly I was being asked to appear as a celebrity guest at after-dinner speaking events. Winning that award catapulted me into the stratosphere of famous female sports stars from nowhere. But there is no manual about how to adjust to living your life under the spotlight. I remember Jonny Wilkinson talking about the guilt that he felt for all the attention he received after the England men's team had won the 2003 World Cup. His extra-time drop-goal had won the match against Australia, but he felt he'd just been doing his job within the team. I knew that my teammates should have been equally recognised but, knowing that I had a profile to effect change, I felt a responsibility with it.

It wasn't long afterwards that I received a phone call from Paul Vaughan, who at the time was chief executive of the organising company that was delivering the 2015 men's World Cup in England. He asked if I would consider being an ambassador for the tournament, along with Jonny Wilkinson, Will Greenwood and Lawrence Dallaglio.

I was honoured to be asked, but at the same time felt awkward about promoting the men's World Cup, when so few people knew who I was. But how could I turn it down? It was the first time a female had been asked to promote a men's World Cup.

The 2015 tournament promised to be a thrilling experience that would boost rugby's profile and hopefully popularity for the game among both sexes. Of course I would do it, I told Paul. It was the period in my career when I just felt grateful to be asked to do anything. To be involved with three legends of the game was enough in itself.

But what I didn't realise is that the other three were being paid, and handsomely so, for their ambassadorial duties, whereas I had been asked to do it on a voluntary basis. I would never have known about this discrepancy until Paul left his role by mutual consent in September of 2012 and was replaced by Debbie Jevans. Debbie had been headhunted after she had received widespread plaudits for her role as director of sport for the London Olympics. Ian Ritchie, the RFU chief executive at the time, was keen for her to sprinkle some London 2012 stardust over the Rugby World Cup. The pair had worked together at the All-England Lawn Tennis Club, where Ritchie had been chief executive and Jevans was a member of the club's committee of management.

But it was a tough job for Debbie. She was a woman without any rugby background or experience and faced hostility from some who no doubt wondered what a former female tennis player knew about rugby. But she was a role model for me. She had reached the top of sporting administration and was not afraid to take herself out of her own comfort zone, something that would become important to me later in my career. She was a visible leader for me at a time when people would at times question what I knew about rugby, to my face and no doubt many more times behind my back.

I could have easily hidden away from my ambassador duties. It was at times intimidating to walk into a rugby club and see the reaction of the members to Jonny, Will and Lawrence in comparison to the reaction that I received. Not many people wanted to hear my anecdotes about our World Cup campaigns – and at times we enjoyed a beer as much as they did – but everyone wanted to hear about the 2003 World Cup triumph. Most of the time I don't think it was sexism, but I did feel invisible. But seeing Debbie front up helped in a way for me to overcome my anxiety.

One of the first things she did when taking up office was also to address the issue of the inequality of my ambassadorial role. She called me in for a meeting to discuss how things were going on. 'It's brilliant that you are involved as one of the four ambassadors, Maggie,' she said. 'Did you know that the others are getting paid for their roles?'

'No, I didn't,' I replied. To be honest, even when she told me, I was not bothered. I would have done the job for nothing, just to be involved.

'Don't worry, it's fine,' I added. But Debbie was having none of it.

'No Maggie, this is NOT fine. It's not acceptable to pay men to do a job but ask the woman to do it for nothing. I'm going to sort this out and make sure you are paid.'

Debbie did sort it. She would become my mentor. It was one of those moments in life when you realise that you are entitled to ask for your fair share. It was an impactful lesson. I still don't know if I got paid the same as the men, because I didn't ask them. But Debbie said she would make sure I was paid fairly.

'You need to recognise you are significant,' she added. 'This is not just about principles, but you have a role to play. You're not just a face for this tournament, but you will be on the road, going around rugby clubs up and down the country. You'll have a platform and unfortunately you'll meet some people who don't think you should be there, and we have to support you to show them why you should.' I left the meeting with a different perspective.

Up to that point, I'd just felt grateful to be part of it. I would go to clubhouses and stand at the side while everyone asked to be photographed with Jonny Wilkinson. But when the odd person asked to be photographed with me, I made sure to make a fuss of them.

When I was next on the road with the Rugby World Cup trophy tour, I made sure that rather than linger in the shadow of Jonny Wilkinson, I'd step forward and make my presence known. I had nothing to hide. I was, as Debbie, said: *significant.* She taught me to be a visible leader too for all the girls and women at those clubs who were looking for inspiration. The key was to show others that rugby could be a game for them.

If a black girl with a club foot from a single-parent family in Edmonton could make it, so could they. Women could be more than just the partners of a significant other who played rugby. They could be players themselves, and experts on the game too.

The activities ramped up once we hit the 'one year to go' mark and some of them were bizarre and entertaining in equal measure. On one occasion I found myself in the front row of what turned out to be the largest scrum in the world, when 1,008 people came together on the pitch at Twickenham. It made the *Guinness Book of Records*.

Later I can remember finding myself climbing Scafell Pike in the Lake District with Sir Bill Beaumont, who was then the RFU chairman, and Ian Metcalfe, a board member of England Rugby 2015, the World Cup organising company, to stage the 'highest line-out in the world', bringing the trophy with us.

Get out of your comfort zone, Maggie, I told myself, time and again during that year. That courage stemmed from the fact that I felt I had equality and had become a valued member of the team of ambassadors. And I have Debbie to thank for that.

****

As if to underscore her commitment to me, Debbie also asked me to be involved with the draw for the World Cup, which became infamous for resulting in England, as hosts, ending up in the so-called 'pool of death' along with Australia and Wales.

It took place in the Tate Modern art gallery in London in December 2012. Boris Johnson was still Mayor of London at the time, still basking in the glow of the Olympics that summer and delivered a bombastic speech to launch the event before the draw. But otherwise, he did not seem too bothered. It was a well-rehearsed set-piece event he could probably do with his eyes closed.

The line-up to pull the balls out of the bowl were Boris, Debbie, Will Greenwood, Richie McCaw and myself.

We were all given strict instructions on the process. When you pick up the ball, read the name of the country, say it loudly and clearly and then hold it up for three seconds before putting it into the slot, we were told. It sounded simple but in truth it was nerve-wracking.

I found myself standing beside Richie McCaw, the same guy that six years earlier I had shared the stage with to collect our IRB awards. I remember thinking that he didn't remember who I was, but it didn't matter. He was delightfully polite, and we chatted away until the official ceremony started and the butterflies in my stomach returned. The imposter syndrome returned too. I looked at the assembled crowd of coaches, dignitaries, sponsors and the media and could not help but wonder if they actually knew who I was, never mind what I was doing up on the stage.

My nerves were not helped by the gasps from the auditorium as England were lumped together with Wales and the Wallabies, and unfortunately they wouldn't make it out of that pool three years later, the first hosts not to do so. Thankfully, though, the blame could not be levelled at me, as my selections were for the final placed sides in the pool. I am not sure, though, that was any consolation to England head coach Stuart Lancaster.

That amazing World Cup journey would take me from the Tate Modern to 10 Downing Street, and tea with the Prime Minister, David Cameron, and the as yet untold story of the broken Cabinet Room chair.

As part of the Rugby World Cup tour, we had to bring the trophy to the UK's most famous address. The trophy was safely housed in the back of a Land Rover, who were one of the main tournament sponsors, which had been specially designed to showcase it, protected by bulletproof glass. The presence of Martin Johnson, England's 2003 World Cup-winning captain, in the car would have been enough of a deterrent to any would-be thieves.

We were to deliver the trophy to the Prime Minister and then stage a photoshoot outside Downing Street. We had to stop at the gates at the end of the road and were met by armed police officers who escorted us in the car. As we got out in front of No. 10, suddenly the door swung open and out stepped the Prime Minister. All I could do was smile. *What I am doing here?*

But the best was yet to come. After the photo opportunity we were ushered into the world-famous Cabinet Room, which has witnessed some of the most monumental moments in British political history.

The Prime Minister ushered us to sit down around the famous table on these beautiful antique oak chairs. Then, just as we sat down, there was an enormous crack. I am not sure they had been built to withstand the weight of former England rugby captains, certainly not Johnno's 6ft 7ins and nineteen-stone frame!

Thankfully the Prime Minister saw the funny side. 'Martin, these chairs are over 200 years old, and you have just gone and broken one,' he said with a laugh. At least it also broke the tension. We all had a chuckle. Johnno would have been inside

No. 10 after England won the World Cup in 2003, but I was still pinching myself. I am sitting with the Prime Minister in the room where cabinet meetings are held every week and all the big government decisions are taken. I was already in awe of travelling in the car with Martin, never mind having tea and chatting with the PM.

We had been accompanied by a member of the World Cup organising company and Cameron made it clear his support. Remarkably, it felt like we were a high-powered delegation from another country seeking support from the UK Government, not a couple of rugby players.

'Okay, what else do you need to make sure this tournament is a success,' he asked. 'You will have my full support.' *Wow, is this really happening?*

Then we went for a walk around the building, looking at the portraits of the former Prime Ministers hanging on the wall by the staircase and exploring the beautiful walled garden out the back. History everywhere. I just never would have imagined that I'd have been allowed into such an historic and important place when I was growing up on a north London housing estate. And then we were gone. But not forgotten. I would have two more meetings with my new mate David Cameron, and I must have made some sort of impression, because next time he would remember me.

****

The same cannot be said for Princess Anne. At least, I hope she doesn't remember me!

First, let me explain the full story, which goes some way to understanding the cognitive dissonance I was experiencing at the time, and ultimately prevented me from walking away from rugby, even if it meant enduring the most humiliating moment of my life in Buckingham Palace, standing in front of the Princess Royal.

The questions I'd begun to ask myself about my future in rugby in the aftermath of the 2010 World Cup wouldn't go away, and the distractions and glamour of the accolades that started to come my way chipped away at my commitment. *Was it worth all the effort to go again for the next tournament in France in four years' time?*

I didn't know what more we could have done in the previous World Cup cycle. And with my public profile rising in the months afterwards, I started to wonder if it was time to do something completely different. I knew the attention I was receiving wouldn't last, maybe it was time to seize the moment?

Several of my closest friends on the team, including our captain Catherine Spencer, had also decided to retire from the game. She told me at a training camp before the start of the Six Nations, along with Katy Daley-Mclean, who would take over the captaincy, Gary Street and Graham Smith. I knew what a tough decision it was for her and she broke down in tears telling us her news.

We won the 2011 Six Nations Grand Slam without breaking our stride, but the media attention from the World Cup had all but evaporated. All the focus was back on Martin Johnson's side ahead of their World Cup in New Zealand later that year.

I didn't know if I should keep going. My low mood continued through the year. I kept playing but during our final Six Nations match of the 2012 campaign, a 23–6 victory over Ireland at Esher that secured a seventh straight championship title, and a sixth Grand Slam for us, I suffered a nasty knee injury.

Rachael Burford, our centre, made a tackle and, as they swung around, I received a heavy knock to my knee. I couldn't play on, and a scan later revealed I'd torn my meniscus.

I needed an operation and was out for a number of months. The only consolation was that my rehabilitation coincided with the London Olympics, which allowed me to devour every minute of the coverage. But it was during this time that I felt so low that retiring from rugby seriously crossed my mind. I was close to depression.

My mum had also found my passion for rugby strange, so it wasn't as if I had a big parental influence insisting that I should keep playing, the way a father might urge his son to do. I'd been out of the game for so long and around me the world was moving on.

Then, one day, as I was moping about the flat feeling sorry for myself, I got a text from someone at Saracens amateur rugby club, saying that a letter had arrived for me at the club and it might be a good idea if I came to pick it up because it looked 'official'.

Looking back, it was as if fate had intervened. It had been such a horrendous day that I barely had the motivation to open the letter. But I did. Perhaps it was because it looked so important, as on closer inspection it had been embossed with 'HRH'.

It informed me formally that I'd been awarded an MBE in the Queen's Birthday Honours list and asked if I would accept it. The letter also requested that I go for a security check before they could officially announce it. So, they vetted me and I was terrified that they would discover a couple of parking tickets and rule me out.

I was in the clear. It turned out that I'd been nominated by a former player who I'd made a big impression on in the community, which made it even more special. Another letter arrived to inform me that I was due to collect my MBE from Buckingham Palace, but it didn't specify who I would receive the award from. I naturally assumed that it would be from the Queen.

I took three guests, Emma, a close friend of mine from college, my partner at the time and my mum. I was told I could drive there, so I took my big Ford, with rugby balls and tackle shields in the back, and drove up to the side of Buckingham Palace. My car was checked before the gates opened and I was able to drive into the main courtyard of the palace. I remember suddenly feeling a burning sense of shame that I hadn't cleaned the car for the big day. There were still splashes of mud streaked across it from the many visits to rugby clubs across the south-east of England. It would turn out to be the least of my worries.

We were greeted by a courtier and then my guests took their seats and the recipients of honours had to go to a different room, where we had tea and biscuits. The only chat in the room was discussing who we thought would be handing out the awards. The general consensus was that it had to be the Queen. Then the atmosphere was pierced when one of the courtiers knocked at the door and came in to announce that today we would be receiving our awards from . . . Princess Anne.

I would love to have met the Queen, but remember thinking: *Okay, cool* when we heard the news. The problem was that in my naivety about the royal family, I didn't know much about the Princess Royal's background.

We were then informed that the ceremony would involve us walking up to Princess Anne. We would perform a curtsy, and then she would talk to us for roughly three minutes. Once she was finished, we were told she would stick out her hand for us to shake and then we would curtsy again before following the courtier out of the room.

That sounds simple enough, I thought to myself. The entire ceremony would last around three hours, a bit like a university graduation. I was intrigued to know Princess Anne knew all of our back stories, but it turned out the courtier would prompt her. The problem for me was that I had nobody by my side, prompting *me*.

The first issue, however, was my outfit. I'd bought a dress for the occasion and a fascinator for my hair. Everything was fine apart from my shoes, which, I only discovered as I attempted to walk through the palace, were too big. I stuffed some tissues into them to try to make them snugger, but I started to panic as I was instructed to follow the courtier to take our place for the ceremony. It was a long, long walk and my shoes were falling off. My toes were grabbing at the soles of my shoes to keep them on.

Before I reached the Princess, I looked over at my guest party only to see Emma mouth to me: 'Your mum's asleep!' It had been a long wait, and I felt for them. I mouthed back to Emma: 'WAKE HER UP!' Thankfully the message was received and with a couple of elbows to her side, Mum stirred just in time to see me receive the award.

My name was called out by the courtier to come and collect my MBE. 'Dr Maggie Alphonsi.' Mum had time to stir from her slumber because I was so worried about stepping out of my shoes, or worse trip, that I approached the princess with a painfully slow walk, like a John Travolta strut in the film *Staying Alive*. I could see her looking at me, wondering what I was doing.

It would go from bad to worse. I curtsied but then her first question caught me off guard. 'What are you a doctor of?' she asked.

I froze. It was true, I was a doctor, of sorts. I'd been awarded an Honorary Doctor of Arts by the University of Bedfordshire in 2010 for services to rugby.

I think she was genuinely intrigued, thinking I was a doctor of medicine.

I panicked. Flustered by my ill-fitting shoes, my mum's catnap and standing in front of the Queen's daughter, my brain would not compute what to say.

'Er,' I mumbled. 'I'm a doctor of rugby.' As soon as I said it, I immediately felt stupid. I meant to say it was an honorary doctorate for my services to rugby. But it was too late. Not surprisingly, an odd look came across Princess Anne's face. She was no doubt thinking: *A doctor of rugby, what on earth's that?*

If the hole I was standing in was already deep, I was about to keep digging. In my naivety, I didn't realise that Princess Anne had connections or interests in the fields of the people who were receiving awards, including rugby. She'd been the patron of the Scottish Rugby Union since 1986, having opened the stadium's East Stand three years earlier. Her daughter, Zara Phillips, was married to Mike Tindall, the former England centre and World Cup winner in 2003.

I should have known all this. But instead, I blurted out probably the most stupid thing I could have said next in what no doubt seemed a patronising manner question. 'Do you like rugby?' I asked.

There was that odd look again. 'I do hope so,' she replied in a stern voice that I would describe as 'royal'. 'I am the patron of the SRU, and my daughter is married to Mike Tindall. I am also a proud and devoted Scotland supporter and try to go to every home game. Yes, I absolutely love rugby.'

All I could do was shrivel up in front of her. My three minutes, the most embarrassing I have ever experienced, at least came to an abrupt end when she put her hand out as if to say, 'I am done with you now.' That was the signal. I curtsied again and said my thanks, and shuffled off in utter humiliation, consoled only by the fact that no one else, apart from the courtier, had heard our conversation.

I hope Princess Anne can forgive me now. Our exchange didn't go as I'd intended. And what she won't know is that it was during the course of that unforgettable afternoon in Buckingham Palace that I made my decision to cast off thoughts of walking away from rugby.

It's not often that you get recognition like that while you're still playing and if that made me think again, my conversations with the other people receiving honours that day confirmed it.

I was blown away by what the others had achieved. 'I shouldn't be here, you guys are amazing,' I said to one of the groups on hearing their stories. But their reaction surprised me.

'Maggie, what you are doing is amazing,' one woman said to me. 'You're an inspiration for young people to get involved in sport and be healthy and have an active lifestyle. You're doing something special, even if you think you're not.'

Elite athletes tend not to look beyond their own personal targets and goals, but the words hit home with me. I'd never thought of what I was doing as impactful on others. Sometimes you need someone to remind you of that.

I may have left Buckingham Palace in my muddy Ford estate with my tail between my legs, but by the time I reached home, my personal goals had been reset. Not only would I keep playing, but I had two years to improve my physicality, tactical awareness and technical skills in time for the World Cup in France in 2014. And I'd never felt more motivated.

FIFTEEN

THE STATE OF THE UNION

The incorporation of the RFUW into the RFU was rightly regarded as a momentous day. And not just because I was finally now allowed to work inside Twickenham, rather than the portacabin in the north car park.

The RFU board also established a 'Womens and Girls Integration Board' to ensure that both the grassroots game and our England elite set-up continued to receive the appropriate focus through the governing body. Deborah Griffin, the former chair of the RFUW board, became chair of the new integration board. Ian Ritchie, the RFU chief executive, made all the right noises on the historic day in July 2012.

'We are very much looking forward to combining knowledge and resources and to welcoming new colleagues from the RFUW,' he said. 'This is a progressive move to make the Union even more inclusive going forwards, with our ultimate aim to broaden the reach of the game to the widest possible audience. Joining forces with the RFUW will allow us to do that.'

Sadly, the words were not backed up by deeds. In those early years at least. Within a year I'd left the RFU, my drive and passion to grow the game tainted by the toxic environment.

I guess, to be fair, the integration was always going to take time. It also hadn't been helped by the meltdown in the corporate governance at the top of the RFU the previous year. It had been a turbulent time. It had begun with arguments at the top of the RFU over the appointment of a performance director.

John Steele had been appointed as the RFU chief executive in 2010, the successor to the long-standing Francis Baron. There was an expectation that Sir Clive Woodward, England's World Cup-winning head coach, would return to Twickenham as performance director, but the recruitment process led to a breakdown in his relationship with RFU chairman Martyn Thomas and his chief executive. I had a lot of time for John and the work he'd done previously with UK Sport. But I felt he was treated badly and he was eventually sacked after just nine months in the job. The fall-out from the controversy escalated and eventually Thomas, who had taken over as acting chief executive, was forced to stand down as chair of the board.

Bewilderingly though, Thomas remained as acting chief executive following Steele's departure. It was a hugely demoralising time for the staff. Where was the corporate governance? It could never happen nowadays, but the RFU was in such a state back then that Thomas could be forced to step down as chair and then find himself in an even more powerful and salaried position as chief executive. It is one thing chairing a board, but running the RFU requires completely different skill sets and experience.

I remember being called to a staff briefing and Thomas spoke to us, reassuring that everyone in the room was valued for their roles. 'I even say "hello" to the lady at reception,' he said, giving the impression that he didn't even know her name. It was as if he was trying too hard to show he cared. It didn't seem to wash with the staff.

I remember everyone coming out of the meeting and people were saying: 'Are they f****** serious?' There was huge uncertainty about our jobs, and we lacked confidence in those at the top. Pretty much everyone wanted to jump ship. I was starting to fall out of love with my job.

The mood inside Twickenham only deteriorated when the off-pitch controversies emerged during the men's 2011 World Cup in New Zealand, with players caught up in a series of incidents from attending a dwarf-tossing event to jumping off a ferry in Auckland harbour. England crashed out at the quarter-final stage with a defeat to France and Martin Johnson became the next big figure to resign.

The appointment of Ian Ritchie as chief executive and the start of Stuart Lancaster's tenure as England head coach, first as interim for the 2012 Six Nations and then permanently to the 2015 World Cup, at least brought a breath of fresh air – and normalcy – to the organisation.

But morale was still low, and I was experiencing increasing tensions as I tried to combine playing for England with my role as a divisional talent development officer. I had a lack of confidence in my line manager at the time, and a slightly tricky relationship with my head of performance, Nicky Ponsford. We were both in a ridiculous situation really. She was in overall charge of my day job and also my on-field performance with England. It created a conflict of interests. My immediate line manager was Tom Stokes, who went on to become team manager of the England men's team and the British and Irish Lions. The problem was that I had two identities: Maggie the England player and Maggie the RFU employee. Every time I went to play for England in the Six Nations it felt like I wasn't doing my job and that slowly soured the relationship with both Tom and Nicky.

The situation wasn't helped when Tom left to take up his role with England and was replaced by Andy Paton, who was one of the divisional talent development officers. It was tough. There were frustrations because he was good friends with Tom and it felt like he was just handed the job. It summed up the culture at the time.

Our Six Nations matches coincided with the men's games at that stage and I remember being told that I'd be rested for a match against Italy so that I could attend my duties with the RFU. My male counterparts were full-time professionals, earning over £15,000 per Test match at the time, and yet the same governing body that was supposed to be overseeing my elite programme was also asking me to forgo an international cap for the day job.

I was furious. I was missing out on caps for England to go and work for the RFU. Can you imagine how frustrating that was? Some would ask why I didn't leave the job then, but I loved my work supporting the talent pathway and the development of the future Red Roses. Also, the senior leadership at the time (Nicky, Tom as well as Andy) appointed me knowing my England commitments and aspirations. Even now I look back and wonder at the number of caps I had to miss out on because I was working for the RFU. We might have merged but the playing field was far from level. If I'd been working for another governing body or high-profile organisation, I believe it would have been a different story. I'd believed that working for the governing body that oversaw rugby in England would mean that I would be supported, but that wasn't the case. Some of my teammates had given up their jobs, like Spencer, going into the 2010 World Cup, and now I could see why. It felt so unjust.

I felt there was a breakdown in trust too, that I was constantly being watched to see if I was doing things that were not to do with my role but were more associated with my rugby development. The conflict of interest between my job and being an England player was becoming overwhelming. I was being made to feel guilty for representing my country. I remember a time being told that if I didn't commit fully to the job then I wouldn't be selected for England. I was taken aback by the threat, that my inclusion in the England squad was even being discussed.

I was then rested for another Test match, against the USA, and I knew the higher powers that be were influencing my involvement within the squad again. My mind was made up. It was a game we would win convincingly, but that wasn't the point. I should have been playing or at least involved in the squad, but because of the level of opposition, it was assumed that I wasn't needed and would be better served giving time back to my RFU role. I couldn't go on like this. I had to leave what I'd first perceived to be a dream job.

It was such a shame because I loved working with the young players, such as Alex Matthews, Zoe Harrison, Sarah Bern and Jess Breach. I knew how important visibility was. Liza Burgess had shown me the way when I was a troubled kid more interested in fighting than learning. If I hadn't asked how she got a black eye one day, I would never have even known about rugby. God knows where I'd be now. But the lines were too blurred. I'd lost faith in the senior leadership. I'd had enough. I needed to go. I felt that I'd given my all to the job and went above and beyond to serve the community game and the England Women's talent pathway, but the feeling wasn't mutual at the top. I had to make a choice and my commitment to playing for England was absolute, even if that meant stepping away.

It was a crystallising moment for me. Any thoughts of retirement had already been banished but I also realised that the accolades I'd received were, while amazing, also distractions on my path to what was my third goal: to win the World Cup. I draw on this experience when I give leadership talks to businesses: the importance of focusing on your goal and acknowledging distractions but letting them define you. There would be plenty of time when my playing career was over to cherish those awards, but for now I had to ignore them.

I went to see Andy. It was the biggest decision of my career to walk in and tell him that I didn't want to work at the RFU anymore. It was also a big risk for me personally. I would be giving up a £30,000-a-year job and my beloved company car (upgraded from a Ford to a Volkswagen Golf estate), stuffed full of rugby balls and tackle bags.

I think he was expecting me to kick off, as our relationship had started to sour, and so I think he was quite surprised when I just told him I was quitting. I think I surprised myself as I had no job to go to. I'd started to build a relationship with the Youth Sport Trust, which would eventually lead to a new job, and the RFU would later offer me a full-time playing contract to join the England Sevens programme. It was a mistake that almost all the big unions made at the time following the decision to make sevens an Olympic sport, starting with the Games in Rio in 2016. Everyone started chasing medals and the funding that would come with it, but it came at the expense of the fifteen-a-side programmes. The women's game at the time wasn't big enough to support both and consequently England suffered in a way that would eventually catch up with Ireland. In the 2013 Six Nations, we would meekly surrender our crown, finishing in third place after heavy defeats by Ireland and France.

But for now, as I walked out of Twickenham stadium having handed in my notice, my only emotion was relief. I walked into town, getting a coffee from the Starbucks opposite Twickenham station.

'Oh my God, I've done it!' I said to myself and then allowed myself a smile. I had no regrets. Instead, it felt like a huge weight had been lifted off my shoulders. It was one of the happiest moments in my career. I loved playing for England but working for the RFU had been dragging me down. Now I'd cut the strings and felt free again. I knew I had to find another job, and quickly, and it wasn't long before other opportunities started to turn up. John Steele, the man sacked by the RFU, had taken up a job as chief executive at the Trust. I already had a relationship with the Youth Sport Trust and was approached to take up a role as a Sky Sports Living for Sport athlete mentor, which involved going into schools, mentoring the students and developing their skills. I felt so enriched. I was able to facilitate the development of young people again.

I met some incredible students. I recall one amazing young man called Wayne Instrell. I met him during a visit to a school in Bedford. I was delivering a rugby session and sharing my story to his class. He then approached me after the session to tell me that he loved rugby and his dad also loved rugby. I was so pleased to see that this young man had taken to this sport during my visit. I then suggested to him that he should go to his local rugby club and give the sport a go. The same way Liza Burgess did for me many years ago, which ended up changing my life.

Following the session I spoke to his teacher, Mr Cox, to better understand what Wayne's story was. He then informed me that Wayne had been on a tough journey; he'd previously been bullied and was taken out of mainstream school to receive the necessary support. He then regained his confidence but, just as he was getting back to his best, his father passed away. At that moment, I felt like our paths had crossed for a reason. Wayne went on to be named Sky Sports Living for Sport Student of the Year that year, receiving his award from Dame Jess Ennis-Hill and David Beckham, a tribute to the significant progress he had made. His confidence grew and he went on to deliver motivational talks about his journey to other young people, showing them that anything is possible. Now a grown man, he works in broadcasting, frequently mixing with sporting stars. His journey and resilience inspired me. It made me appreciate that I'd made the right decision to leave. Then a job came up at the organisation to be an athlete mentor manager. I had to go for it.

It was meant to be. I got it and my salary jumped to £40,000, albeit without a company car this time. My time was spent between Loughborough and London, and this time no one was looking over my shoulder. I had a brilliant line manager called Shaun Heathcote. For once I was able to thrive, rather than just survive.

When Steele left as chief executive, Ali Oliver replaced him and she was a joy to work for, along with the chair, Dame Sue Campbell, who is now director of women's football at the Football Association. Both were inspirational women and were my role models at the time; they drove me to push beyond my boundaries and follow my passion.

It had been a tough year. But I was back on the right track. Ironically, it would be letting go of the RFU career that would also prove to be one of the seminal moments in my playing career.

SIXTEEN

WINNING THE FIGHT

My departure from the RFU allowed me to focus fully on the recovery from my knee injury, which was so problematic that it would sideline me for twenty months and leave me facing the biggest fight of my playing career.

There were times when I feared it was a fight I'd lose. In the dark moments when I was rehabbing on my own, I feared the worst. I'd been coping with physical problems since I was born with my club foot, yet paradoxically, for most of my playing career, I felt physically invincible. Of course, I picked up the odd injury along the way, but I never felt like I was a player who'd been constantly dogged by injuries.

But this was one of those injuries that every player hates, one that refuses to heal with any sense of linear progress and would get worse before it would get better.

In my ignorance, I first thought the tear to my meniscus that I sustained during our victory over Ireland in March 2012 would, at most, be a three-month injury.

The initial plan was to attempt rehab without the need for surgery, following the scan. I was told that healing would be a challenge because of the lack of blood to that part of the knee, but given the complications of surgery, we should avoid it if we could. Other athletes had recovered some similar meniscus tears without going under the knife.

But instead of improving, my injury got worse. I was referred to see Mr Andrew Williams, one of the world's foremost knee surgeons who has operated on Premier League football stars as well as international rugby and cricket players. I was very lucky to be able to see him. We took the decision to go for the operation, and his reputation was such that I had faith that I'd be able to play again – although I admit I was still anxious before the procedure. I'd hoped I'd be able to recover without it. When I had the club foot operation, I was so young I had no memory of it. The second operation, on my Lisfranc injury, had gone okay, but I remember my comeback from it being a challenge, feeling like I had to learn how to walk properly again and strengthen the muscles in my foot after a period of inactivity. This one felt like it would be an even bigger challenge. I always had a thing about knee injuries. I can remember hearing people talk about them, saying that if you had a bad one, your career could be over. Would I ever be able to play again? And, if I could, would I be able to get back to my best? It was a very significant joint and I knew there were no guarantees.

But I knew that Andy was one of the best surgeons and I put my faith in him. The operation went well, but the road to recovery was hard.

In the first weeks, I was still working at Twickenham for the RFU, and, unable to drive, I was getting picked up by my former England teammate Nessie Gray every day.

I felt vulnerable, even more so in the final toxic days of my time at Twickenham. As I hobbled about on crutches, I wondered if I'd ever return to the stadium as a player once I'd called time on my RFU job. I felt alone. I was still technically an England player, but now one without any teammates. My rehabilitation was a singular challenge. I knew my back was against the wall, but I knew also that I was the only one who could solve the problem. *Trust the process Maggie, put the work in. You'll be fine.*

There, at the back of my mind was my mum's voice again: 'Maggie, you've got to work damn hard to be successful.' She had drummed it into me from a young age.

The Olympics at least took my mind off my worries, although watching those glorious nights on the television, including Super Saturday when in the space of forty-four minutes, Mo Farah, Jessica Ennis-Hill and Greg Rutherford won three gold medals for Great Britain, as wonderful as it was, it also left me acutely aware of my own incapacity. I was still predominately living at home with my mum and, although she tried to offer support, I still had low moments. In fact, everything felt low. The thing that I loved I couldn't do. It's always remarkable how we take our bodies for granted, until they stop working.

Of course, I wasn't alone. I may have missed my teammates during my recovery period, but Andy had given me a time frame to work to. And I received amazing support from the English Institute of Sport. Dan Howells was my regional strength and conditioning coach for north London and he was brilliant. He would go on to work with the England women's fifteen-a-side team before joining Wasps in the Premiership. We devised a plan to ensure I returned fitter and stronger than I had ever been.

I also had a 'rehab buddy' in Nolli Waterman, who was also injured at that time. We'd spend many of those lonely hours together, sitting on the Watt bikes at the country club gym at Bisham Abbey. We'd chat and offer each other support. She was my rock and looking back I hope she knows how much that time meant to me.

I was used to customised conditioning programmes to compensate for my club foot, which involved strengthening my right-hand side, and when doing any form of weights exercise, making sure I was balanced and my technique was good as well as compensating for my left-hand side so it wouldn't cause me further problems down the line. My constant goal throughout my career was to make sure my muscles on the right-hand side of my body were equal to my left.

But it was a long, hard journey. The 2014 World Cup was coming on to the horizon, but at times it felt like a long way away.

****

My comeback would be further complicated by the offer of a full-time contract from the England Sevens squad. These were uncharted waters for the women's game. The World Cup Sevens was due to be staged in Moscow in June 2013 and the RFU, seemingly chasing the goal of Olympic medals in Rio in 2016, made another significant investment in the sevens programme.

It was lovely to be included. I'd enjoyed our sevens sojourn in Dubai in 2009. I was in the process of returning to play when the offer came, but my knee was still not 100 per cent. Looking back now, I should have turned it down. I was not really a sevens player but, having missed so much rugby in the previous year, and to be given the opportunity to be a professional athlete, I was desperate to be involved and most of my teammates had also been selected for the sevens squad too. The impact would be long felt.

Again, looking back with the benefit of hindsight, stripping the fifteen-a-side squad of seventeen players ahead of our Six Nations campaign was hard to comprehend, just over a year out from the World Cup in France. Claire Allan, Heather Fisher, Kat Merchant, Natasha Hunt, Rachael Burford, Katy Daley-Mclean, Emily Scarratt and Marlie Packer were among the players who were called into the sevens programme.

It seemed like a strange move. The previous autumn, England's fifteen-a-side team had beaten New Zealand 3–0, part of Gary Street's strategy to ensure that we played against the Black Ferns more often in between World Cups. As impressive as it looked, it didn't take into account the fact that New Zealand had sent over a weakened side because they had started prioritising their sevens programme following the 2010 World Cup in England. They'd lost the sevens final the previous year to Australia. Canada were another side to make sevens their priority, along with Australia, but they had all started much earlier than England.

The frustrating thing about the Black Ferns is that it didn't seem to matter what they did in between World Cups, they would just turn up every four years with a really strong squad and win it.

With England, it felt like we'd got ourselves caught between two stools by only prioritising sevens at the start of 2013 – too late to have a real impact on our World Cup campaign in Moscow and too close to the fifteen-a-side World Cup the following year. It also created unnecessary tension between the two squads, with the priority given to the sevens.

The immediate impact was felt by the fifteen-a-side team in the Six Nations. We had won the previous seven titles, but in 2013 we finished in third place, behind Grand Slam champions Ireland and France. We'd lost to Ireland 25–0 in Ashbourne in Leinster and 30–20 to France at Twickenham. Ouch.

My knee would have prevented me from taking part in the Six Nations anyway. Although I was able to train with the sevens squad, I had to keep dropping out until a showdown with our team physio, Julia Headingly, called time on my hopes of playing in the Moscow tournament and continuing my participation in the sevens programme. The training was actually putting my recovery back. To pursue my dream of playing as a professional athlete, I'd been playing with it strapped up, but was causing further damage.

Julia is a great physio because she calls it as it is. She is not there to be your best friend. But I hated her at the time for what she said. 'Maggie, you need to quit the sevens programme and focus on fifteens to give yourself the best chance of playing in the World Cup next year,' she told me. 'Your knee isn't going to be right for sevens, you're only making it worse. Go and get your knee right. I think you should leave the programme.'

I just remember thinking: *How dare you? I've done everything I possibly can. I will be fit. I will be fine!*

We'd met in Bisham Abbey, where the sevens squad was based. I loved it there. Rubbing shoulders with other international athletes, such as the GB hockey team, who were also based there, was so inspirational.

I became good friends with Alex Danson-Bennett, the GB captain and Helen and Kate Richardson-Walsh. Some of the Great Britain rowing team were also based there. I couldn't help feeling a sense of insecurity, however, because of my injury. To be blunt, at times I felt like a fraud. Yet I didn't want to say goodbye to it all. The squad were already out training by the time my meeting with Julia had finished. I just left. That was it. I didn't even get to say goodbye. Bisham Abbey is a beautiful grade one listed manor house at the heart of fantastic sports facilities in Berkshire. I still remember walking down the gravel driveway to my car, climbing in and bursting into tears. I felt like I'd let myself down and squandered my first opportunity to be a full-time professional rugby player.

But there was Mum's voice again. *Maggie, you've got to work damn hard to be successful.*

As I wiped the tears from my face and turned the key in the ignition, I drove off vowing to show Julia that I'd be back to my best and in the greatest shape of my life for the 2014 World Cup. It had given me a new focus to get my hands on the winner's medal that had so far eluded me. That, after all, was my ultimate goal and I owe Julia for reminding me of that. I will forever be grateful to her for being straight with me and not protecting my ego. The sevens had once again been a nice distraction.

And as it turned out, the investment and commitment of full-time contracts didn't have the impact the RFU had hoped it would on England's performances in Russia. We finished second in our pool behind the hosts before crashing out of the quarter-finals with a thumping 24–7 defeat by New Zealand, and then lost to Australia in the final of the plate and finished in sixth place, when in 2009 we finished fifth, which showed just how much other nations had advanced.

****

I spent the summer months continuing my rehabilitation at Loughborough as my role with the Youth Sport Trust became full time, now that my rugby contract had come to an end.

Julia had been right. If it hadn't been for her, I probably wouldn't have made it to the 2014 World Cup.

The twisting and turning and bursts of acceleration required for sevens had not been good for my knee. I wouldn't have changed anything despite all the challenges because it would all give me greater focus.

I knew my knee was never going to be as good as it once was, but by building the muscles around it, I was told I'd have at least one more year of playing fifteen-a-side rugby. I missed England's forgettable summer tour of New Zealand which resulted in a 3–0 Test series defeat (another hangover of our sevens policy), but returned to action with Saracens in September 2013.

By the time my England recall came in November, with an emotional return to Twickenham for a seismic encounter with France, I felt in great condition again. The knee was strong again and my sense of invincibility had returned.

Running out at the stadium never felt so good. I'd put my RFU troubles behind me, even if it felt strange returning to my former workplace. But what meant everything to me was the moment I stepped back on to the famous turf. I hate to recall how many times I'd feared I'd never make it back during those twenty months out of the game, and how many times I'd been close to calling it a day. We were seeking revenge for the humiliation of losing to them here in the previous season's Six Nations. I was seeking revenge for twenty months of hurt.

I'd spent the summer and the early months of the new season testing my knee, taking hits and running at people, being tackled by others. Club level was a different level of intensity to Test matches, and it was the perfect proving ground for me. My target had been to be match-ready by the France game as I knew that if I hadn't returned by then, my hopes of making the World Cup squad the following year would be seriously jeopardised as the coaches would start pencilling in their squad. Marlie Parker was starting to come into the fold and my main competition for the jersey, Heather Fisher, was still very strong, and another Saracens teammate of mine, Hannah Gallagher, was another name who was pushing hard for a place in the England back row. I knew time was against me and this was my moment to prove to Gary Street that I was back.

Only a few thousand spectators remained after the men's international against Argentina, but it mattered little to me.

My sixty-fourth cap turned out to be one of my best performances for England. I almost scored within twelve minutes only to be held up over the line, with Kay Wilson scoring seconds later when the ball was recycled. My try came soon after Claire Allan slipped a pass to move after a following move to the right-hand side. I had been tracking her after I had put her in space. She took on their fullback and I was inside, running with my hand half up as if to plead for the pass. Claire is both a great passer of the ball and, thankfully, a very unselfish player. She returned the pass and I grasped it out of the air, without breaking my stride to score from about thirty metres out. After twenty months of darkness, exhilaration coursed through my veins. It was my greatest try, if I'm honest, even though it wasn't *my* try. I'd just finished off a great team move but it meant way more to me than five points. There were a number of great flankers who'd emerged during my time away from the game, all of whom could have made compelling cases to start for England ahead of me. I knew there had been a chance I wouldn't wear the jersey again. To do so at the home of England rugby and to cap it with a try was special.

We won the game 40–20 and in the changing room afterwards I reflected on my performance. My body felt great. And what's more, I'd played with a freedom that I hadn't experienced since the early years of my England career. I think perhaps that the final months of my time with the RFU had dragged me down on and off the pitch and as a consequence I hadn't been enjoying my rugby as much. Maybe my injury had come at the right time, despite everything that I'd been through. The result was that I now had a completely different perspective as lots of things had changed in my life.

****

My feeling of elation back in the white shirt wouldn't last long, however. England were able to select from a full panel for the start of the Six Nations in 2014 now that the sevens programme was over. Yet there appeared to be something of a hangover because the reintegration wasn't as smooth as it could have been. The girls who had been away with the sevens had to reset their playing styles to the fifteen-a-side game and it would take a while for the rhythm and instinct to return to the team. As for me, the feel-good bubble from the victory over France would pop in the most spectacular fashion as we opened our campaign against the French again at the Stade des Alpes in Grenoble.

Throughout my career, the Six Nations always boiled down to a decider between England and France, a decider that we would invariably win. That was until 2014. We lost 18–6, which should have set alarm bells ringing at the start of the World Cup year. In 2003, Martin Johnson's side romped to a spectacular Grand Slam in their Six Nations campaign on the way to their World Cup triumph in Sydney later that year. In contrast, we'd stumbled, badly, at the first hurdle.

From one of my best performances in an England shirt, to one of my worst. I had a shocker. I told myself afterwards it was because I'd been trying too hard to prove myself. There was one moment that summed up my day. I made a break and was charging towards their fullback, Jessy Tremouliere. There was only one thought in my mind: *I'm going to gas you!* What had I been thinking? I think Emily Scarratt was on my inside and if I'd passed to her it was a certain score. But I had no intention of passing. I wanted to underline the point that I was back. And then I was tackled. A try then could have swung the game back in our favour.

But as a team we made a lot of uncharacteristic errors. I barely slept that night in the team hotel. For some reason I had a room to myself – we usually shared – and being on my own made it worse. My autumn return had gone to plan but now with the clock ticking down to the World Cup in France, something just didn't feel right. My anxiety was heightened by the fact that I knew this was going to be my last World Cup, my last shot at a winner's medal. I lay on the hotel bed, wishing I could curl up into a little ball.

Gary and his coaching staff put together their analysis for our review session the following morning. It wasn't long into the team meeting that my error came under the spotlight. 'So, Maggie,' said Gary. 'Shall we just let this bit of play run for a bit.' *Please don't, Gary.*

It looked even worse in slow motion. It's one of the joys of being an elite athlete to see the mistake that had kept you awake all night, played back again in a video session along with all your teammates who were no doubt thinking to themselves: 'Well, why didn't you pass it, Maggie?' I took it on the chin. 'Yeah, fair play, that was my bad,' I replied. Another thing being an elite athlete had taught me was to own your mistakes.

Maybe it was because I had played so little international rugby over the last two years, but my performance was so bad that it rocked my confidence to the core. Maybe I wasn't as good as I thought I'd been against France in November. Maybe I should have retired when my knee injury was at its most troublesome.

But I had to keep telling myself that one bad game did not make me a bad athlete. The problem was that I felt that I *was* a bad athlete. I am pretty sure that my teammates thought that they were bad athletes too.

Our next game was against Scotland, and I feared the worst. My mind shot back to my first cap, and how I felt when I was dropped after that and cast into the wilderness. If I was cast into the wilderness now, my World Cup dreams might be shattered for the last time.

And I was cast into the wilderness. Well, sort of. I was dropped from the starting XV to face Scotland at the Rubislaw Playing Fields in Aberdeen. Cheers, Gary. I guess I deserved that one.

But by the time we travelled north, my mind was already back in a good place. The game against France had been played in front of a decent crowd with a lot of pressure. The Scotland game would be very different. The venue looked like we were playing in a field. And I vowed to myself that, if I got off the bench, I'd do everything I could to make amends. Gary gave me my chance in the fifty-fourth minute and this time I wouldn't let him down. I managed to score another try in a 63–0 victory. It was exactly the right response, a high-tempo, clinical and ruthless performance. And Gary's tactical genius in dropping me had worked a treat. It was a message to say that while it was great to have me back, more than ever I needed to bring my 'A' game to keep my place in the final furlong of my career. The second message was to remind me that my 'A' game was enough. I didn't have to force things to prove to others – even myself – that I was worth my place in the side.

I received both messages loud and clear. We may not have hit the heights that our male counterparts managed in their 2003 Six Nations campaign, but we didn't lose another game. I was back in the starting XV for our hard-fought 17–10 victory over Ireland at Twickenham in the next game. I remember thinking how much Ireland had improved since I'd last played against them and they would push France all the way in their final game at the Stade du Hameau in Pau. France held on 19–15 but Ireland had demonstrated that their victory in last season's Six Nations wasn't a one-off. None of us could have known then how significant their rise would prove later in the year.

I scored again in a comfortable 35–3 win over Wales at the same stadium two weeks later and we finished our campaign with another one-sided 24–0 victory against Italy at the Stadio Giulio e Silvio Pagani in Rovato, Brescia. France finished as champions, with us two points behind in second place. It wasn't what we would have wanted going into the World Cup. Far from it. We now hadn't won the Six Nations since 2012, when I'd sustained my knee injury (yes, that long!). Yet I couldn't help thinking the championship had been the wake-up call we'd all needed. Most of all, me.

SEVENTEEN

THE TROUBLEMAKERS

Our Six Nations performance had come as a blow to our collective confidence – and restoring it became a key focus of our summer World Cup training camps.

We still felt like we were one of the best sides in the world, and we now had the experience and leadership that I felt we'd lacked in 2010. Yet there were mounting pressures too. We were the richest rugby union in the world, had the best facilities and had the right coaching team around us. We had no excuses now. I'd been on a long and, at times, emotional journey with many of the players in the squad. For many of us, we knew this was going to be our last World Cup. And losing two finals in a row had naturally left some mental scars. That brought the pressure of expectation too. It was now or never.

At least the main benefit of our poor Six Nations campaign was that there was no risk of us resting on our laurels. And given that so many of us had been to World Cups before, we knew it would be a completely different kettle of fish in France than the Six Nations, because the pressure would be on to perform in every game.

With greater investment from the RFU, we would have more time together as a squad and the message from the start was: we can turn this around. It was a hugely intensive camp. We spent time with the Royal Marines in Portsmouth and also played behind-closed-doors training matches against the USA and Wales. They were full-on games, made tougher by the fact that players could be rolled on and off. We nearly lost to the USA. It was another jolt to the confidence. I couldn't understand it. We were fit, confident in our game plan and with an experienced coaching team. *Why weren't we clicking?*

In the quiet moments away from the squad, I was concerned that if we didn't improve, I knew we could find ourselves hanging on by our fingernails during the World Cup. There was a slight concern that the sevens may have had a detrimental impact. It was hard to transition back. We had some big names who went to Moscow and there was bound to have been some lingering mental hangover from the fact that they didn't achieve the goal of winning that World Cup. I can remember Heather Fisher saying that she effectively had to relearn how to be a fifteens forward again – how to ruck, maul, hit breakdowns and navigate around more players, having been used to the ball coming to her in sevens and then given the freedom to attack into space.

In some ways, I was lucky because my knee injury had effectively brought me back into the fifteen-a-side set-up earlier. With sevens being introduced into the Olympics in 2016, it remained a distraction beyond Moscow. Canada, ominously, were the one country who had invested in their sevens programme first and then reintegrated their star players more quickly into their fifteens programme.

The one ace up our sleeve, however, was our sport psychologist, Cherrie Daley. I'd always enjoyed working with psychologists ever since I'd joined the England squad. But working with Cherrie was transformational. It was far from an auspicious start, however. When she came into the squad, she identified me as one of a group which we felt were being labelled as the 'Troublemakers'.

I was blissfully unaware, thinking only that I couldn't wait to start working with the new sports psychologist. Then I remember having a meeting with her, along with a few of my teammates, including Tamara Taylor, Katy Daley-Mclean, Claire Allan and a few others. I couldn't work out why we were seeing her. We later found out that it was because we'd been picked out as senior players – characters and leaders – in the squad and that she needed to get our buy-in first. It felt like we'd been wrongly branded as the 'Troublemakers' because we had a voice and influence – but that was because we'd been around the squad for a long time.

Whatever the thinking behind the move, it didn't go to plan. If anything, it made the 'Troublemakers' feel more antagonised and even ostracised. It was a lesson learned. Cherrie may have started off on the wrong foot. But she would prove to be the final piece in our jigsaw to give us a winning edge.

To be blunt, she wouldn't take any s***. And was to the point. She was lean and had a field hockey player's build. Even though many of us towered over her in height and size, she wasn't afraid to call players out if she felt they weren't telling the truth. She'd frequently say, 'No BS.' She wasn't a rugby player, so she had no baggage or any sense of ego. She put us in our places when we needed to be put there. After the slightly stumbled start, she quickly recovered and began to make a real impact, starting with our coaches. She spent a long time with Gary and Graham, getting to know them first and how they operated before getting to know us. It was the right way to do it, because developing the mindset of the players only works when the coaches are aligned.

She put a huge focus on developing our culture and ethos and above all putting the team first and getting our buy-in. What really impressed me was that she captured everyone's attention. Some coaches see sport psychologists' work as something to be tolerated or just as a box-ticking exercise, but Gary and Graham fully bought into her ways – and that says a lot about her because they were tough cookies.

During our camp there would be dedicated sport psych sessions. Some coaches might have thought that it was a wasted session, a time when we could have done a speed or fitness session or rugby skills instead. But Gary and Graham made sure we had dedicated time within our programme and within our camps for Cherrie to work with us. The sessions focused on building and strengthening the team, creating a culture that everyone bought into and establishing a bond between players (and staff) that couldn't be broken.

I remember doing an 'insight' session – a psychometric tool that's often used in business to improve self-awareness and understand team members' strengths and leadership styles. The assessment would help each player find out what 'colour' they were. Each colour represented a different personality trait. During one session Cherrie got us standing in a circle and asked someone to stand in the middle. 'Right, what's her colour?' she would ask us of our teammate standing awkwardly, looking at her feet. 'What personality trait does she lead with?'

There were four colours: red, which meant you were likely to be task-driven and got to the point; yellow meant you had a sunny character and were more likely to be sociable; green people were empathetic and caring about others; and blue were deep-thinkers and would assess the detail before acting (very opposite to red!).

I was red. *Of course I was.* What the exercise achieved was far more than just identifying personality colours. It shone a light on what made each of us tick. It brought us closer together and gave us a better understanding of each other as people, not just players. And what I loved about it was that she extrapolated this information and pieced it together for best use in a team environment. Cherrie was interested in us as individuals but overwhelmingly saw her job to make us more effective as a team unit.

Rather than saying: 'How do we help Maggie the athlete?' She was more interested in finding out ways of making us a team capable of winning the World Cup through better interaction as teammates.

Question followed question. 'How do you understand each other? How do you become closer as a team? How do you bond as a team?'

I'd been used to being asked: 'What does Maggie Alphonsi need to get better?' Cherrie instead was asking: 'How can the team best support Maggie?' And consequently, 'How can Maggie best support the team?' and 'How can we as a team complete a task?' In the process, she made us feel quite vulnerable. I'd never felt vulnerable before with other sports psychologists. Maybe me talking as an individual with them, but never before with my teammates. Previously my vulnerability might have been to say that I didn't feel fit enough, or I was worried about my pass off my left hand. But this was different. This was a vulnerability where we had to share our family situation or what our life goals were. I had to open up. People who know me will recognise that I do not always find that an easy thing to do. At heart, I'm a private person.

It worked a treat. Katy Daley-Mclean, one of the original 'Troublemakers', had emerged as a fine captain. Her tactical brilliance and coolness under pressure would spread confidence throughout the squad when the pressure came on. And with Cherrie's work through the summer, we would set off for France with an unbreakable band of sisters' spirit. What we could not have known was that Cherrie had one final ace up her sleeve.

****

Gary Street had put us through the most brutal pre-tournament training camp I'd ever experienced. No player I knew ever looked forward to pre-season training, but our preparation for this World Cup took this sense of dread to a whole new level. The training days with the marines in Portsmouth weren't as mentally challenging as our three-day camp with the army in the Brecon Beacons four years earlier had been. But that would prove to be a false dawn.

Gary, like all of us who were heading to our third World Cup, had changed as a head coach. Maybe evolved is a better word. There was a steeliness about his approach now. Previously he'd always been a lively and entertaining character, the type of bloke you'd want to be your best man at a wedding. He could balance a chair on his nose, for example. But between 2010 and 2014, Gary changed. He retained his fun side but after the pain of our defeat to New Zealand in the 2010 final he revealed a new serious side too, as if to say: *We need to get the job done.*

I can remember a soul-searching meeting months after the 2010 final. He asked us why we'd come back. At first, none of us knew what to say, but at the end of the meeting he handed out Post-it notes and asked us to write down exactly why we wanted to keep playing for England. Some themes emerged. We all felt we'd underachieved in 2010; we were desperate for women's sport to grow but had missed a golden opportunity; we'd not fulfilled our potential and we wanted to be ambassadors, trailblazers even, for those coming after us. In the white-hot moments of the World Cup, we would draw strength from remembering exactly why we had come back.

His new approach manifested itself in two ways during our World Cup camps. Firstly, we would make sure that, whatever happened, we would go to the World Cup as the fittest team in the tournament. There would be no excuses. I knew how tough the pre-seasons had been before the 2006 and 2010 World Cups.

But in 2014, when we were based at the Surrey Sports Park, it felt like the objective was to break us. I couldn't help but feel anxious. This was my third World Cup. It was going to be my last. And I knew we were going to get beasted.

Tuesdays were the worst day. I think Gary called them 'Toughen-up Tuesdays'. We frequently did a lung-busting anaerobic shuttle test. It was effectively the evolution of the old 'bleep test' relevant for sports that were very interval by nature. It didn't just test the upper limits of our conditioning, but it was also a mental test. Who wanted it more? Who would keep going when they felt like they had nothing left to give?

We would undertake the test in our units, and the back row, made up of Sarah Hunter, Heather Fisher, Hannah Gallagher, Marlie Packer, Alex Matthews and myself, was always the most fiercely contested. We were ridiculously competitive. We were fit and athletic and just went hard at each other. I was usually paired up with Fisher or Hannah. Hannah was my protégé. Like me, she had started at centre and then switched to the back row and also played for Saracens, and I'd coached her when she was younger. She was a fantastic specimen, a brilliant athlete who was making her way. I was in good shape too, but had experience on my side. It made for a relentless battle. We'd become good friends and knew how to push each other. Sadly, when it came to the final cut, Hannah didn't make the squad bound for France, but she had played her part as my training partner.

Fisher was the queen of the anaerobic shuttle test (and she annoyingly had pace as well – she had previously been on the British bobsleigh team), with Hannah and myself pushing each other hard for second place. We ran so hard there was no time to think. It involved putting a first cone five metres out from the touchline, then putting another cone ten metres out, then fifteen metres, twenty metres, twenty-five metres and, finally, thirty metres. Out to five and back, out to ten and back, and so on.

The aim was to do as many shuttles as possible in thirty seconds. Then you had thirty seconds rest, before going again for another thirty seconds. It lasted for six minutes, working with a partner who would run when you were resting. It doesn't sound much, but it was brutal. We would all stand and cheer on the different units until it was your turn. The secret was to walk back while you recovered to get to the baseline as quickly as possible. Some girls would get their breath first at their finishing cone and then had to rush back before the thirty seconds rest had concluded.

The way Gary and Graham had set it up, they created fierce competition, but it also encouraged us to inspire each other. No one wanted to let the others down. Gary and Graham kept monitoring our body language. I remember our strength and conditioning coach, Stuart Pickering, was brilliant at punishing us if we showed poor body language during a fitness session. If anyone put their hands on their knees, he would make us do the whole session again, even if we were absolutely hanging. As well as getting us fitter, they were also testing us mentally and psychologically. It defined our camps. While I loved the challenge, I still remember doing my last session before we left for Paris and feeling an overwhelming sense of relief.

To win a World Cup, we had to navigate through five games in seventeen days. At least we knew that if we failed, it wouldn't be because of our fitness. And there was something reassuring about that.

But Gary wanted us to also be the best team under pressure. Sir Clive Woodward, who coached England men to their 2003 World Cup triumph, famously used to use the T-CUP concept to coach pressure. It stood for: Think Correctly Under Pressure. Gary's approach was to focus on: What if?

We talked in depth about our 2010 final and how we'd failed to capitalise when New Zealand were down to thirteen with two players in the sin bin. We'd not managed the situation well.

Then, when we went behind 13–10 with just minutes to go, Gary said we'd been too cautious. We'd made the tackle and then stood off, rather than piling in when we had nothing to lose and attempting to pressurise New Zealand into making mistakes. Gary had been to a neuroscientist to learn how the brain worked under pressure and said that the female brain tends to react by resulting in risk-averse behaviour in these situations, while men react by 'going over the top'. His plan since then had been to put us all under pressure at different points and at different times so that when we got to game-time, it felt much less stressful than training.

He'd hit us with scenario after scenario for what he called 'consequence training': what happens if our captain and fly-half Katy Daley-Mclean is injured during a match? Who would step up? What if we lost our hooker or main lineout caller? What if Gary or Graham were not available? How would we manage training?

Then one day Gary didn't turn up. We looked around, expecting to spot him hiding in the trees, watching to see how we would react in his absence. 'He's at it again with another one of his "what if" games,' somebody said.

It turned out that on his way to training his mother had called him to say his father had just had a heart attack. He drove straight to his parents' house and then the hospital. It was exactly the sort of scenario he had planned for. We got on with our training and shared our sympathies with him when we found out his absence had been for a real emergency. He knew then we were ready.

****

As we headed to France, my mind headed back to that phone call from Gary, when he'd asked me to come and join his England Academy squad after the devastation of being dropped after my first cap. He'd worked with several of us since we'd played for age-group sides and had travelled with the squad for our first World Cup in Edmonton. The bond couldn't have been tighter. We'd all grown up since 2010, collectively become smarter players and coaches, and we'd all become better decision-makers.

If Gary had changed over the course of the last four years, so had I. The experience in Edmonton had been exhilarating. I'd been young, naive and free from fear. Four years later, I'd relished being in the Olympic village spirit of the Surrey Sports Park and breaking the glass ceiling for the women's game at The Stoop.

Now, I was in a very different state of mind. If the previous two tournaments had an amateur feel about them, I felt a newfound sense of seriousness as we headed to France. I was on duty for my country. I was here to do a job, a mission to achieve and there was nothing that was going to stop us from reaching our goal.

When we arrived in Paris, the immediate change from the previous tournaments was that we were allocated our own hotel, making it feel more like a men's World Cup. Well, almost. After a few minutes we discovered the USA team were also staying there too. But I didn't mind. I always had a soft spot for the Americans. Their players had a certain awe about them. They were all big athletes – most of them looked like heptathletes – and one of their players, Jillian Potter, in particular would be such an inspirational figure for me, coming back from both a serious neck injury and then from a rare form of cancer. We were respectful of each other in the hotel and, unlike 2010, we had own area to eat and had our own team rooms, a sign of the increasing professionalism of the tournament.

Otherwise, we remained pretty much in our own bubble. Gary's attention to detail ensured that instead of training at the tournament base in Marcoussis, he hired a local rugby club which had been fitted out with the same gym equipment and paraphernalia from Twickenham. We travelled there each morning from our hotel in two minibuses. It would be a home from home.

Until, that was, we faced a challenge that not even one of Gary's most wild 'What If?' scenarios could have prepared us for.

One morning, when we arrived at our training pitch, we found a handful of police waiting to speak to us. They'd been there every day, but had previously remained in the background. I'd often wondered why they were there. Now I knew why. A group of armed travellers had arrived overnight and taken up camp around our pitch. Our team manager, the legendary Janette 'Jan Man' Shaw, was calm as ever and said, 'Don't worry, we'll sort it.'

But we were told that there was nothing that could be done to evict them. Gary would later be fined during a court session for failing to prepare us for training while surrounded by armed travellers. But he'd prepared us for getting on with things. And so we trained with several police officers standing guard on the touchlines. It was surreal. Gary would later say that the police showed him bullets they'd picked up from some of the caravans.

Then, at the end of the session, the police officers came over and asked if they could get their photograph taken with us. I have to say I never felt threatened. In contrast, the interest shown by the French public in the tournament made it feel like people were starting to take a real interest in women's rugby. We would be stopped outside our hotel for photographs, while articles constantly appeared in the French press.

One morning Tamara Taylor pointed to an article in one of the newspapers. 'Maggie, you get a mention,' she said. Tamara was fluent in French. 'Can you read it to me?' I asked. She did so with relish. I still don't know if she was making it up, as I don't speak any French, but she said, 'England have a very good rugby player called Maggie Alphonsi.' I'll take that. All of the games attracted great crowds as well. We had set the world record for our final in 2010, but here every game seemed to have caught the attention of French rugby supporters.

There were moments of old-school amateurism. We rarely had a day off, but on one occasion that we did have a few hours off I decided to meet up with some of my Saracens teammates who had travelled out to Paris. We'd been told we had to be back at the hotel for a certain time that afternoon, so I jumped on the Metro to meet up with them at the Eiffel Tower. Time passed and suddenly I realised I was under pressure to get back in time. By chance I bumped into Nolli Waterman's mum, who offered to give me a lift to training. It was a lovely gesture, but the only problem was that we quickly got lost. I started to panic. There was no way I was going to get back in time for our forwards session, which was being taken by Graham Smith. If Gary was like your best man, Graham was like your angry uncle. I didn't want to tell him. I phoned Jan Man instead. Sorry Gary, on this occasion, I decided the path of least resistance was the best one to take.

'Jan Man, I am lost in a car with Nolli's mum, can you tell Graham I'm going to be late for training?' I said.

'Alright man,' said she in her calm Geordie accent. Jan Man was never panicked.

But I wasn't out of trouble. As I rushed to the pitch uttering my apologies, Graham shot me a withering look. You never wanted to disappoint him or push him too far. I'd learned my lesson. This wasn't the time to go sightseeing with your mates. We were here to win a World Cup. Graham's glare told me everything I needed to know.

EIGHTEEN

'THANK YOU, MISS'

It was always a freshly cut rose. Even when we weren't allowed to wear the rose emblem when representing England, as we hadn't been able to during my first World Cup in 2006, the player who was making their debut would receive the real thing during the jersey presentation ceremony on the night before our games. As a gesture, I found it incredibly moving.

After your first game for England, the ceremony was more traditional, receiving your cap from the captain or head coach, and having to sing a song on the team bus on the way back from the post-match function. But receiving the rose before the game added to the sense of occasion.

Each rose comes with a player number. Mine was 111. It was a thing of beauty. Afterwards I got it pressed and kept my rose for many years. Indeed, I hope it's still in a box somewhere up in my attic.

By 2014, women's rugby was already unrecognisable from that day in 2003 when I won the first of seventy-four caps for my country. But thankfully this unique part of the ceremony remained constant. Any time a new player came into the team, watching their eyes light up when they received their rose would bring back memories of how I felt the night before my first cap.

Some of my teammates might laugh at hearing such sentimentality. Maggie? Is that you Maggie? Are you okay, pet? I can hear them mocking me right now. I get it. I was never one for showing much emotion during my eleven years as an England player.

But that didn't mean I didn't feel emotion behind my wise-cracking persona. And now, sitting in the rather nondescript function room that doubled up as our team room in our Parisian hotel, my mask had well and truly slipped.

At the front of the room stood Jan Man, as she'd done so for most of my caps. No one received a rose that night, but I was already crying by the time she started calling out our names in turn to go up and receive our jerseys from Gary and shake hands with her and the rest of the management team who were all lined up. I waited for my number to come up.

'Number seven is Maggie Alphonsi,' said Jan Man. I cried every step to the front of the room and then proceeded to hug every member of staff for as long as I could. I'd done this seventy-four times, shaking people's hands and saying thank you.

I'd only told a handful of people that this would be my last cap, so the rest of the squad must have wondered what was going on when my crying turned into a proper, snorting blubber as I returned to my seat. I looked up, embarrassed, to see if anyone was looking at me.

I guess everyone must have known my secret. It's a moment that will stay with me forever, that bond of emotion in the room. It had been a remarkable journey. Old players had moved on, new players had come in, others, like Hannah Gallagher, were knocking at the door. But right then, in that moment, we embodied all the strife, effort and resilience required by the women and girls playing our sport, often against the odds, across the country.

I knew my body couldn't go on, even if I'd wanted to keep playing. I'd probably known at the start of the season, but I didn't want to make an announcement then as it would have defined my season. The enormity of the situation overwhelmed me. But by game day, I was back in the zone, with no thoughts of retirement. I had just eighty minutes of my England career left. Just eighty minutes left to achieve my lifetime ambition to win a World Cup . . .

****

The truth is, I shouldn't have been in a position to do so. Despite all our efforts of the previous three months, we hadn't been at the top of our game in Paris. I'm not sure I can honestly say we deserved our place in the 2014 final at the Stade Jean-Bouin, my third successive final, and my last.

I look back now and wonder if it was a mix of the fear of missing out for a third time in a row? I certainly think that pulling the squad in two directions because of the sevens programme the previous year had not helped. There were probably at least two occasions when our journey should have come to a premature end. It doesn't bear thinking about, but the odd time I get a flashback I shudder at the thought.

The start of our campaign had been positive. We'd romped to big wins over Samoa (65–3) and Spain (45–5) in our opening two pool games. The results were misleading, as our final pool match against Canada at Marcoussis would reveal. To progress to the semi-finals, we had to finish among the top four sides, ranked first according to their position within their pool and then by competition points.

Canada were a team that we at least knew lots about. I guess I knew more than most because at the time I was in a relationship with one of their players, their inside-centre Mandy Marchak.

We'd first met when she came over from Canada to play for Saracens in 2011. She was one of the rising stars of Canadian rugby and part of their sevens programme as well.

It had been a long-distance relationship because she had to return to Canada for several months each year to be part of her sevens programme. I would travel over to see her in Vancouver Island, once in the summer and then once in winter. But ahead of the game, we had stopped speaking to each other. She went from being my best friend to my worst enemy.

Playing against each other made the relationship feel awkward. I got a bit of stick from my teammates, but because she played her rugby in England with Saracens, she was good friends with a lot of players in our squad. She was a nice person and a great athlete. But what was important to me was that no one ever questioned if I would go easy on her because she was my partner. In fact, it was the opposite. I think we both wanted to make that point. It's like when brothers or sisters play against each other in separate teams and want to smash each other.

We were both respected athletes in our respective teams. I knew she was a quality centre, an influential player on the Canada team and she had to be stopped. I look back now and think that it was a strange situation to be in. But during the 2014 World Cup, it only made my focus more intense, not less.

Whether it was a personal distraction or not, collectively we were just not right. We'd played Canada many times and beaten them so I guess we perhaps lacked the extra edge mentally that we should have had going into that was effectively a quarter-final match. There's no doubt that we underestimated them.

That wasn't an issue for me. In fact, it was probably the opposite, because of my relations with Mandy. I think my performance was affected by the desire to try *too* hard. I ran about the pitch trying to make big tackles. After one hit, I received a deep cut just above my eye and had to go off for a few stitches. I looked like a boxer. When I came back on, the chaos continued. I remember shouting: 'What the hell are we doing?'

My answer to the crisis was to up my work rate. I made more tackles in that game than any of my previous caps. There was an element of fear that drove me on. It felt like our World Cup hopes were hanging by a thread.

It was Emily Scarratt's trusty boot that kept us alive. She kicked two penalties in the first half to give us a 6–5 lead at the break to cancel out a try by Karen Paquin by Canada.

But it was far from convincing. When Kayla Mack scored a second try for Canada, their lead was deserved. It brought back memories of my first World Cup, when it took a brilliant cover tackle by Kim Shaylor to prevent Heather Moyse from scoring the winning try in our semi-final against Canada in 2006.

This time our 'Kim Shaylor' moment came from a massive England scrum that resulted in a try for Sarah Hunter to put us back in front. But Canada hit back with a penalty to Magali Harvey to snatch a 13–13 draw. We had been bloody lucky. But it was enough to ensure we topped our pool on points difference, but we had to thank Ireland for ensuring we qualified for the semi-finals.

Their historic 17–14 victory over New Zealand was the first time a senior Ireland side – men's or women's – had beaten New Zealand. And it proved to be remarkable timing for us. The Black Ferns, for so long our nemesis, were out. I couldn't believe it. In the four years preceding this tournament we'd planned to play them as many times as possible, in preparation for that moment when we would meet again in a World Cup final. We did all the homework, but we didn't plan for an early New Zealand exit. I guess Ireland beating New Zealand was another 'what if' moment, but one we had totally overlooked!

It's hard to put into words how I felt. I guess relief was my overriding emotion. At one stage I can remember doing an interview with Sara Orchard from BBC Sport straight after the match and fearing that we wouldn't make it to the semi-finals, never mind the finals.

With New Zealand gone, instead we faced Ireland in the semi-final at the Stade Jean-Bouin. It was tough for them. Beating the Black Ferns had been such a momentous occasion, and must have been incredibly draining, both emotionally and physically. In contrast, we had the attitude of one of the favourites who had just been handed a second chance. That we probably hadn't deserved it made us even more dangerous.

We smashed them. We played our best rugby of the tournament, winning 40–7. Ireland had given their all against New Zealand but seemed to have nothing left in the tank for another heavyweight contest.

And fortune smiled on us again as Canada, buoyed by their draw against us, defeated hosts France in their semi-final. Magali Harvey scored a wonder try from a scrum deep in her own half and yet France could have won but failed to convert two late tries from rolling mauls. As hosts, France had the huge advantage of home support. As good a team as Canada were, they had now had two huge games in succession. And, surely, we couldn't play as badly as we had done against them in the pool stage, could we? It was time for Cherrie Daley to pull off her masterstroke.

****

Before my emotions had got the better of me during our jersey presentation on the eve of the final, the day before Cherrie gathered us together for one last task.

'I'd like you all to disappear off to your rooms and record a message on your mobile phones, explaining why you want to win the World Cup,' she told us. I'd never heard of the 'Why' concept before, but it was a theory born by Simon Sinek, a British-born

American author and inspirational speaker. The essence of the concept is to understand what motivates a person, to uncover what their driver is. In this context, the exercise proved to be incredibly powerful. Why did I want to win the World Cup? I wasn't sure. I guess it was all I'd known since I began this amazing rugby journey. The girl from Edmonton Green had wanted to be a world champion. But why?

The question hung in the air. I thought about everything that had gone on before this moment. The highs and lows, the people who'd supported me along the way. All the hard work and sacrifices I'd made too. I often think of elite sportspeople as being like icebergs. When the supporter sees them in action, it's only the tip of the body of work that has taken them to that point. I took the exercise very seriously and, after hitting the record button on my phone, offloaded my drivers. Firstly, I said, I wanted to win the World Cup for the women who had gone before us. England had won our first World Cup twenty years earlier, in 1994. They'd been our trailblazers. If I thought we'd faced a mountain to climb in terms of gaining recognition for our game, it was nothing compared to what they had endured. The 1994 tournament, the second World Cup, was meant to have been held in Amsterdam, but was cancelled at short notice when the organisers failed to get official endorsement of the event from the IRB. Instead, a rearranged and unrecognised tournament was staged in Scotland to give the women who had trained so hard to participate in the event the opportunity to compete. England defeated the USA in the final, with eleven of the original sixteen countries taking part. The rebel event was a hugely significant staging post for us all. I wanted to do it for them and the 'fantastic four' too. The four pioneering women who started the very first Women's Rugby World Cup way back in 1991: Deborah Griffin, Susan Dorrington, Alice Cooper and Mary Forsyth. If it wasn't for them, none of this would been possible.

I waffled on. I wanted to continue their legacy. Then came the 'why' that got right to my core. My mum. I wanted more than anything to make my mum proud. I looked back at my childhood and thought about the battles she had to fight for me as a single mother from Nigeria living in a tough estate in north London. I thought of the several jobs she juggled to keep us afloat, even if it meant that she had to sacrifice time with me during those precious childhood years. I thought of her determination to ensure I got the right treatment for my club foot. Of her support for me when I had to stand up for myself, of her coming to terms with my sexuality even though it jarred with her strict religious upbringing. I thought of the commitment she made to support my rugby journey, even though it was a sport that must have seemed so alien to her. Mum had given up everything to enable me to have a life. She'd not been able to travel to Paris, but I knew she would be watching at home, back in the flat where my life had begun. This final was for her.

When we reassembled together the next day, we played back all of our messages on the big hotel TV screen. It was the first time I'd been vulnerable in front of my teammates (my tears had yet to come). That made it even more emotionally powerful for me. If I was a bit embarrassed about the length of my message, I loved hearing the rich variety of 'whys' from my teammates. Some had left funny or witty comments, others very short ones. It was not enough to say, 'I have trained for ten years to get there.' People really dug deep into what had driven them on to reach this moment. That night, I'd never felt closer to my teammates. I felt so inspired. I wanted to win the World Cup for the women in the room and for the women who had paved the way before us. I just knew it, our time had come to take back that trophy.

****

My abiding memory of the hours before kick-off were the French police outriders, who parted the traffic to ensure our coach got to the stadium safely and on time. How I could have done with them when Nolli's mum had been trying to whizz me back from my Eiffel Tower excursion the week before!

It might sound like a small point. But having a police escort made it feel like it was an important event, taking us a step closer to our male colleagues, who had been used to such VIP treatment for decades.

There was a genuine sense of occasion about the final too. The French supporters turned out, despite the disappointment of their side's semi-final defeat. Officially it was a 20,000 sell-out at the Stade Jean-Bouin and, although a sizable section had turned up to see France defeat Ireland in their third/fourth place play-off match, many of them stayed on to watch the final. A lot of our supporters jumped on the Eurostar. It meant so much to me that many of my Saracens teammates had made the trip.

The game itself was another fraught affair. No wonder. There were eleven players who had appeared in the final four years earlier in our starting XV. We were a team made up of plumbers, vets, teachers, police officers and students and many of us had taken three months' unpaid leave to represent our country.

We had so much to lose against a Canada side that was playing in their first final, free from the mental baggage that weighed heavily on our shoulders.

I did my best to run around and knock over their star players, including Mandy (our line of communication had stopped again), but while we'd significantly improved on our pool performance against them, we could not repeat the intensity of our victory over Ireland in the semi-final. In fact, it was Canada who had the best of the chances in the opening period – Magali Harvey was a constant threat.

Perhaps it was appropriate that it was left to Emily Scarratt, the wonderfully talented centre playing in her first final, to deliver the match-winning performance.

She kicked two penalties in the first half to put us 6–0 in front, while Natasha 'Mo' Hunt had come agonisingly close to a try but was adjudged to have been held up just short of the line.

Nolli Waterman, my old rehab buddy, appeared to have put us clear when she scored our first try before the break. She finished a fine move in style, with Tamara Taylor finding space with a cheeky dummy and the years of studying running lines of the world's best No. 7s meant that, when it mattered, I was on her shoulder. A simple pass was enough to give Nolli the space she needed to finish.

We were in control. Or so we thought. Magali Harvey, who was the women's world player of the year, had missed a couple of kicks in our 13–13 draw, but here she was immaculate, landing three penalties to drag Canada back into the contest. At 11–9, it was anyone's game, and they could tell that the pressure was mounting on us. New Zealand had turned the screw in a similar fashion at The Stoop four years earlier.

But our mental resilience was more robust now. Emily kicked another penalty to restore our lead to five points before delivering her *coup de grâce*, stepping powerfully inside to elude a tackle attempt by Mandy before slicing through the cover defence for a brilliant solo try. When she added the conversion, our celebrations could start early. At 21–9 there was no way back for Canada; our twenty-year wait to win the World Cup was over. That was for you, Mum.

****

At the final whistle, I turned to embrace my back row teammate Sarah Hunter. She is one of the finest forwards this country has ever produced and would go on to captain the side, playing in two more finals and finishing her career as England's most capped rugby player of all time, with 138 caps. But right then, in that moment, she was my mate, my back row mucker . . . my fellow world champion! We jumped in the air and embraced other teammates, with relief coursing through my veins. 'We've done it, we've DONE it,' I screamed. Not dissimilar from the famous moment when England men had realised they had won the Rugby World Cup in 2003 in Australia and Jonny Wilkinson and Will Greenwood were jumping up and down embracing each other shouting, 'We've won, we've won!'

The pain on the faces of the statuesque Canadians quickly brought back the memories of how I had felt at the final whistle of the 2006 and 2010 finals. I went to find Mandy to console her and then each of her teammates. I made a point of shaking their hands. 'I'm sorry, I know how it feels. Well done, you played well,' I said, over and over again. But I knew my words of consolation wouldn't pierce the pain of defeat in a World Cup final. Winning that final would change our lives forever. But they had missed out on that chance. They knew it. I knew how they felt. I'd stood on the pitch twice before and watched our opponents experience their moment of elation. It is a hopeless feeling. Finishing in second place – and receiving a silver medal – is still a huge achievement. But, in the moment, it feels nothing like it. It is a heartbreaking place to be. The team that finishes third by winning the third/fourth place play-off at least experiences the joy of winning their last match. The Canadians final memory of Paris 2014 was defeat and a list of their own 'what if' questions.

Gary's list had achieved its goal. We had no more questions to answer. This was our moment. It was all happening in a blur. People were on the pitch setting up the trophy presentation platform. My mind shot back to watching the Olympic Games on the TV in my mum's flat as a schoolgirl. My memory was that the British athlete who had just won a medal went to the crowd to get a Union flag to drape over them. I wanted to be like them, so I ran over to the crowd to get an England flag and ran around like Jessica Ennis-Hill with it like a cape around my shoulders.

The Canadian girls went up first to get their silver medals. Understandably, the first thing some of them did was take their medals off their necks as if to disassociate themselves from failure because it was not the colour they wanted. It was not until I retired that I felt I could take out my two silver medals from the bottom of a drawer and actually appreciate what they still represented, a fantastic achievement. I would later have all three medals framed along with my three England jerseys. Those two silver medals all played a part in my journey to finish with a gold medal.

As it was my last game, I was the first to go up to receive my medal and it was great to see a familiar face, Sir Bill Beaumont, among the dignitaries. He'd been at the medal presentation ceremony in all three of my finals.

'Well done, Maggie, you've done it, what a fantastic achievement,' he said. I think some people thought I was the captain as I went up first, but Katy was last on so she could receive the trophy as well. For those few seconds, I didn't know what to do with myself, as I was used to walking off with a silver medal and then standing in a group vowing that we would remember the feeling because we didn't want to go through it again. Because I was the first on to the stage, I ended up in the far corner of the stage. Gary came over to sit next to me after he got his medal and we gave each other a hug. 'We did it. We won the World Cup.' The only problem was that when Katy lifted the trophy and the golden ticker tape rained down on us, we were too far away so barely featured in any of the photographs. I should have positioned myself by the trophy. You would have thought that after seventy-four caps I would have been a bit more streetwise! Oh well.

The entire ceremony lasted around sixty seconds. The greatest minute of my sporting career. When I give leadership talks nowadays, I often refer to that minute. By the time Katy had lifted the trophy and the ticker tape had fallen to the ground, as we stepped off the stage, the stadium was already emptying. It had taken twelve years to get those priceless sixty seconds. The elation may have been fleeting, but I knew then that no one could take it away from us, no matter what happened next.

That was when the feeling of relief returned. I couldn't help wondering how I would have felt if we'd lost the final again. I could give you a list of hyperboles. But I didn't feel ecstatic or over the moon. The truth is that all I felt was relief, followed by a sense of emptiness that the journey was over. It's said that true enjoyment comes from the journey, not the destination. Don't get me wrong, the destination was very special, but now I could see there was something in this. I tried to stay in the moment. 'We've done it . . . take a deep breath and relax,' I told myself.

Before my celebrations could properly begin, Jan Man broke the news no one wanted to hear: I'd been one of the players randomly selected for a drugs test. There were three players from each side and I was one of the lucky ones to be chosen. Of all the days to be chosen, it had to be today. Great! I met the drugs tester, who had to follow me until I gave a sample of urine. 'I'm just going to do a lap of honour with my teammates,' I told her. So she followed me all the way round the pitch, while I posed for pictures along the way. This was one moment I wasn't going to cut short.

I felt it was important to acknowledge my friends and teammates in the stands. It took ages, but it was a special time.

Among those people I embraced was Helen 'Rob' Clayton, my original fierce rival for the No.7 shirt for club and then country who then went on to become my mentor and then a great friend. Her last final had been in 2006. I told her this was now my last one. 'It's the changing of the guard, Maggie,' she said. She had passed the No.7 shirt on to me, I hope I'd done it justice, and now it was my time to hand it on to Marlie Packer.

I made my way back to the drug tester and headed for the toilets. It's not as straightforward as it sounds. Some players are so dehydrated, it takes them ages to be able to pee. The urine also has to be the 'right concentration'. I won't go into any more details, but it took a couple of hours. At least we'd won; the wait was even tougher for the three Canadian girls who were in the room with us.

It meant I missed the immediate celebrations in the changing room, and as we left the stadium on the team bus to head to the official dinner, everyone was in great form, and there was still time for an unofficial detour. The bus stopped at this roundabout near the stadium. Nearby was a pub that had England fans spilling out of it. We saw some friends and families too. 'Right, everyone get off the bus, man,' shouted Jan Man. 'You've got thirty minutes, and then everyone back on the bus, man!' It was a lovely gesture, sharing the moment with those we cared most for and the supporters.

I sent a few text messages to those people who had been so instrumental to my journey. One of the most special ones was to Liza Burgess. 'Thank you, Miss,' I wrote. She'd kept an eye on me through my entire journey, and had often sent me messages of support. If it hadn't been for her guidance – and that black eye that first intrigued me – I may never have found rugby and my life would now be in a very different place.

****

People sometimes ask me if female rugby players like to go drinking in a similar fashion to their male counterparts after matches. I often surprise them by saying: 'No, we're much worse!' Just because we're women, it doesn't mean we sit there and drink half a pint of shandy or a small glass of rosé. You have to remember these are women who are a good laugh, very sharp and who know how to have fun. Especially when we've been away for so long, and it's just you and your teammates. Up to that point, everything had been about the work, the job, the task. Now we'd won the World Cup, it was a time for players and staff to let down their hair. Jan Man was our equivalent to Paul 'Bobby' Stridgeon, the Wales and British and Irish Lions strength and conditioning coach who was the life and soul on the Lions tour videos.

What goes on tour, stays on tour, but let's just say the trophy went everywhere – in the pool, a shower, I think someone woke up with it in their bed tucked under the duvet because they didn't want to let go of it. I loved just seeing my teammates celebrate because I knew just how hard they had all trained to get to that point. My teammates will tell you that I've liked a party in my time. When I was nineteen and playing for Saracens, I got a bit too drunk at the club's end-of-season party and stumbled while we were playing a silly game of musical chairs. I missed the chair and landed face down, forgetting to use my hands to break my fall. In the impact I lost two front teeth. All I can remember is someone shouting to get a glass of milk. 'Put the teeth in the milk, it'll save them,' they shouted. I was still living at home with my mum and at that stage I remember the conversation behind me about who was going to take me home. I think everyone was scared of my mum!

Some of my teammates managed to get me home and the next day I had to go to the emergency dentist. Funnily enough, the milk didn't save my teeth. But thankfully they were able to fix me up with a couple of caps put in. It's a story I look back on now with fondness, but it also served as a warning to me about not getting too drunk (because no one wants to be that person!).

And the night we won the World Cup? I was back in my hotel room in my pyjamas by midnight. I had a couple of drinks, but this night was so special that I wanted to remember every second of it. I made myself a cup of tea, put my medal around my neck and went to bed.

NINETEEN

TOP OF THE POPS

I announced my retirement some ten days after the final, when the media buzz of our World Cup win was still at an all-time high.

The idea to keep the announcement until after the final had been Julia Hutton's, our team communications manager. She'd rightly predicted that the news would have more impact if I retired as a World Cup winner.

Julia had done a fantastic job of promoting coverage of women's rugby through her time with the RFU. By the time I retired she had become a good friend and I remember on our flight back to London talking about what I might do next with my career. 'I'm looking for an agent,' I said to her. It must have planted a seed, because not long afterwards Julia became my agent, leaving the RFU the following year to set up her own PR and talent management company – Jules PR – which specialises in female sports.

It was the start of a brilliant working relationship, which is now eight years strong and I hope will continue for many more. Most agents who manage clients in rugby and look after male players are men. Julia was different. She was a woman who knew the game, the sporting landscape and knew me. She was also one of those strong women who came into my life and was not afraid to assert my rights. Like Debbie Jevans before with my role as an ambassador for the 2015 men's World Cup, Julia was fearless in making sure that in the jobs that followed I would get paid what I was worth and, just as importantly, associated myself with the right brands and media outlets.

Julia's mindset was if a male player was getting paid a certain amount for doing the same commercial or broadcasting appearance, even though I'm not them, I still add value as well and we should not be afraid or apologetic in asking for similar amounts of money instead of being grateful or just happy for being asked to do the job.

But on that Sunday morning in Paris, I didn't know what I was going to do next. I'd known for quite a while that this day was coming, and even though my international career had come to an end having fulfilled my lifetime dream, and we were on the front page of nearly every English national newspaper, there was still a feeling of emptiness. I'd spent the last eleven years giving everything I could to play for England. It was what had defined me.

Gary Street came out following my retirement and said some lovely things about me. 'One of the most pleasing things about winning the World Cup is the recognition that Maggie has had,' Gary said. 'In my eyes, she has been a world champion for the eleven years she has been playing for England. She plays every international like it's a World Cup final.'

I was equally pleased for Gary. I'd worked with him since I was in the England Academy. He had given so much of his life to England.

I remember him recalling that, before the 2010 tournament, both his grandparents had recently died and his wife Helen, who was heavily pregnant, had been suffering with rheumatoid arthritis. He'd been under a lot of pressure going into that tournament and when we lost the final it must have been so tough for him. But he rebuilt us in the four years after, with his 'team first' approach. No one deserved our victory more than he did.

It bothers me that he and Graham Smith didn't get the recognition they both deserved afterwards. Just five months after guiding us to victory, Gary quit his job after being told his contract wasn't going to be renewed at the end of the season. He deserved so much better than that.

I was so pleased to see Clive Woodward receive a knighthood when England men won the World Cup in 2003, the captain Martin Johnson received a CBE and Jonny Wilkinson and Jason Leonard OBEs. The rest of the squad received MBEs. Even Francis Baron, then RFU chief executive, received an OBE. All accolades which were rightly deserved.

I just had high hopes that we would also experience the same. When we won the World Cup eleven years later, only two members of the squad received MBEs, Rochelle 'Rocky' Clarke and Sarah Hunter (who was our vice-captain at the time) in the 2014 New Year's Honours. I already had an MBE so I didn't expect anything but I wanted the whole team to be recognised the same way the men were. There was nothing for Gary or Graham. It just showed how significant the gender gap remained in sport.

The difference in commercial value was also enormous. The England players in 2003 reportedly received a match fee of £3,000 and a £12,000 bonus each for winning the World Cup and their earning ability soared afterwards.

Officially, the total financial reward we received for winning our World Cup was . . . nothing. We were amateurs who made personal and financial sacrifices to play for our country. It came as a nice surprise then that, a few weeks after our victory, an anonymous benefactor donated a generous sum of money to be shared out between us in recognition of what we'd achieved.

Gary was at least named high performance and UK coach of the year at the UK coaching awards in Glasgow and was nominated for the BBC Sports Personality of the Year coach award, but Paul McGinley, the Irish golfer, won it instead for coaching the European Ryder Cup team to victory over America. At least we were named team of the year at the BBC awards and had a great night out together. But even now I can't help feeling that both Gary and Graham should have had their efforts formally recognised. They certainly didn't deserve the treatment they received from the RFU after our historic triumph.

I hope it's not too late. I was really pleased to see that Simon Middleton, who succeeded Gary as head coach in a joint role with the England Sevens team, was awarded an MBE for services to rugby in June 2021, and in the same year became the first women's coach to be named World Rugby coach of the year. Simon achieved great things with England, but what Gary and Graham did should have also been formally recognised, as they had won a World Cup.

****

From nowhere, an email dropped into my inbox. I was about to discover my next goal. It was an email that would change my life.

For the first few weeks after our final, I'd felt rudderless. I can remember telling myself on the night that we won the World Cup, when I was back in my hotel room while the others were out partying into the night, that I'd achieved my goal, now what was next? It was what Mum would have said too. But what? I needed a new purpose in life.

Although I'd retired from international rugby, I was determined to finish the season with Saracens. It was the club where I started. A club I loved and still do. I remember when Alex Sanderson left to take up the director of rugby position at Sale Sharks in 2021, he said that part of him would forever be a Saracen. That is how I feel.

But losing that connection with my England teammates left me with 'end-of-tour' blues.

We had some more formal celebrations, including a visit to 10 Downing Street where I caught up with my old mate David Cameron. He was still the Prime Minister, and I was impressed by the fact that he remembered me from my previous visits, even though I was wearing green trainers. 'Hi Maggie, well done. It's great to see you again,' he said. I have to say I was impressed that he had taken an interest in women's sport. We also got a tour of 10 Downing Street and the walled gardens.

But it was quickly back to porridge. I returned to my day job with the Youth Sport Trust, and it was a strange experience to readjust. They put on an event to celebrate our victory and then it was back to my desk in Loughborough. Even though it felt like our achievement would act as a massive catalyst for change in women's sport, the reality felt very different as I found myself eating lunch in the canteen, wondering about the same KPIs (key performance indicators) that I'd faced before Paris.

Then the email landed, via Julia Hutton. It was an invitation to be part of a choir. But not any choir. The invite was to be part of Gareth Malone's All-Star 'Children in Need' choir. *Wow!* Now that sounded like my next challenge all right, because I couldn't sing! But what an opportunity. Taking myself out of my comfort zone has never been a problem for me, right from the time I hopped on the bus to Saracens when I was thirteen. I feel passionately that it's so important for personal development to challenge yourself. You never know where it will take you.

In this case, it took me to the iconic Abbey Road recording studios in London, where The Beatles had recorded their albums. *What was I doing here?*

I didn't even know who else was going to be in the choir. Even more daunting was the fact that I was filmed by a camera crew from the moment I got out of the car. And what a car. Having a black Mercedes arrive to pick me up from my mum's flat in Edmonton had already made me feel like a Hollywood A-lister!

I was escorted into a room where I would meet the other members of the choir. The first person I saw was Fabrice Muamba, the footballer. He'd started his career at Arsenal, my team, but had been forced to retire after surviving a life-threatening incident when his heart had stopped for seventy-eight minutes while playing for Bolton Wanderers. I was already in awe before I saw the others in the room. Behind him was Jo Brand, the comedian, and the people I knew as Mick and Pam, the parents of Gavin, from the sitcom *Gavin and Stacey*, Larry Lamb and Alison Steadman, and Craig Revel Horwood, the *Strictly Come Dancing* judge. They were all instantly recognisable to me, but I suspect none of them knew who I was. Being true professionals, they were all very polite and at least pretended that they did.

If I felt slightly overwhelmed, it only got worse. For those of you who remember the reality TV show *Big Brother*, it resembled the first night when housemates are introduced one by one. Next came Mel Giedroyc, from *Mel and Sue*, the co-host of *Bake Off*, then *Countryfile*'s John Craven, Radzi Chinyanganya from *Blue Peter*, the EasterEnders actor Nitin Ginatra, Linda Robson from *Birds of a Feather* and Radio One DJ Alice Levine.

The room was full of chatter when the final entrance was Gareth Malone himself. 'Congratulations everyone, you are now part of the All Stars choir,' he proclaimed.

Our first job was to choose the song. Out of the three presented to us, the clear choice was 'Wake Me Up' by Avicii. That was the relatively easy part. Gareth's main challenge was to teach us how to sing. Dear Lord, help me. He was faced with a room full of entertainers (apart from me!) so it was like having a room filled with naughty kids, all misbehaving and not really listening to him. Everyone was funny in different ways. It was time for a dose of reality.

'Okay everyone,' said Gareth. 'I basically have six weeks to turn you into a choir that is going to perform live on national television. Let's go.'

To determine our voice types, we did individual sessions for assessment. Then one day Gareth turned up at Saracens for one of our training sessions. 'Maggie, I want you to sing in front of your teammates,' he said. Oh no. It was embarrassing enough to sing a song on the team bus after a match. But this was much worse. And everyone was stone-cold sober.

I had a go. I sang the song. To be fair I love the lyrics, even if I am not sure I did justice to the song. Gareth asked me to have another go, this time 'without the face'. I'd been pulling a face when I had been struggling to hit the high notes. 'Let's try it again, this time a bit lower,' he added.

And so I did. 'Maggie, you're going to be one of our sopranos,' he declared. I must admit, that sounded rather cool. There were three of us: Mel, Amanda, and me. Mel actually had a lovely voice and was chosen to sing one of the solos on the night.

We practised once or twice a week at a variety of locations where the film crew was as they were effectively making a two-hour documentary about our progress. But Gareth had encouraged us to sing everywhere and anywhere we could, even in the shower. As we got closer to the event, we did a practice event at a community hall and performed in front of a group of around twenty people. The feedback was, shall we say, a little underwhelming.

We also visited some of the charities who were going to benefit from the donations during the six weeks. It was lovely to get to know the other members of the choir. I got quite close with Mel. She was such a nice character, and Jo Brand. Jo was someone I knew almost immediately I could become great mates with. She opened up and made you feel you could go to the pub with her for a few pints.

I kept in touch for a while with Jo Brand and Radzi. It was interesting to talk to Craig as well, although he barely mentioned anything about *Strictly*. The closest I got to stargazing was a trip to the set of *EastEnders*. Larry Lamb had also played Archie Mitchell in the soap opera and one day he just said: 'Come on Maggie, do you want to visit Albert Square?' Of course I did. We walked to the set, which was near where we were recording, whizzed through security and the next thing I knew I was walking past the front of the Queen Vic pub. He was great fun and such a nice guy. He later got a job on LBC and asked me to do an interview on his show.

I was working with people I considered to be famous names in the entertainment industry and ended up being mates with them for the next six weeks.

When we came to perform on the night, the legendary Terry Wogan, who was one of the main presenters on the show, came in to say a few words of encouragement to us. The performance itself was exhilarating, even if I now look back and cringe at my performance. If there was ever proof of the benefit of taking myself out of my comfort zone, it was that night. Even now, when I hear the song by Avicii, I think back to that beautiful moment – singing the highest note I could ever sing!

The following week, I was heading out for a Mediterranean dinner with about ten of my Saracens teammates when we heard on the radio that our song had reached No. 1 in the UK charts. Everyone cheered and laughed in equal measure. They all knew the standard of my singing ability, but hey, I was No. 1 in charts, following in the legendary footsteps of The Beatles! That still blows my mind.

****

It was not long before I was rubbing shoulders with celebrities again. Or perhaps, to be more accurate, dipping my shoulder into a celebrity! The comedian and actor Jack Whitehall, to be precise.

Poor Jack. I don't think he knew what he was letting himself in for when Samsung, one of England Rugby's sponsors, decided to run a hilarious advertising campaign ahead of the 2015 World Cup.

The campaign proved to be a massive hit, winning advertising industry awards. Jack was the star of the campaign, which also featured Martin Johnson, Lawrence Dallaglio, Jason Robinson, Jason Leonard – and me.

The campaign was called 'School of Rugby' and the comedic theme was educating Jack about the basics of the game. It was filmed at Maidenhead Rugby Club and, when I arrived, the 'talent' who were already there were this time reassuringly familiar, as I had met or worked with the other four already. There was also a load of players from Maidenhead RFC. There was no sign of Jack at this stage.

The atmosphere was very relaxed. We had breakfast together, the producers talked through the filming and our scripts and then got into our Samsung rugby stash. I guess to make it more realistic, they didn't share the entire script with everyone. I was told that my section was going to be on 'The Tackle'. No problem, I might not be able to sing, but even though I'd retired, I'd kept myself in good condition. And I still loved tackling.

All I was told was that Jack was going to be discussing something with Johnno and Lawrence and then I was going to make a tackle. That was all the information I received and when I arrived everyone was already in character mode. Johnno had been told to be the serious and stern one (no method acting required!), and Lawrence was the narrator who would guide us through it and Jack brought the dry humour.

I didn't quite know what to make of it. I'd never met Jack before but knew who he was. I'd only recently watched him in the sitcom *Bad Education* and seen him do lots of stand-up gigs. Was I really going to have to tackle him? But then again, this was going to be shown on the telly. I couldn't make it look like I had gone soft on him.

You can find the clip of the advert on YouTube. It still makes me smile.

'The best way to learn is to go out and practise,' Lawrence says to Jack during his tackle masterclass. 'Why don't you go in there and be the tackler,' he adds, before calling me over.

'I'm not going to tackle a lady,' Jack replies.

'This is Maggie, one of our greatest-ever rugby players. Have you got a problem with that?' Lawrence asks.

'Yes, I do, I don't know how you were brought up, Lawrence, but I will not be tackling a lady. That will not be happening today. Sorry Maggie.'

I smile and then Lawrence suggests that we swap around and that I become the tackler. 'I'm fine with that,' I say, with a glint in my eye.

Poor Jack had to first smash into a tackle bag held by Johnno and then run at me. I was up for this. Geoff Richards was back in my ear again . . . 'Make the f****** tackle, Maggie.' If I could tackle Owen Farrell, I could definitely knock Jack over. Smash.

But what you don't see on the clip is how many tackles I had to make. The director, who was also Jack's good mate, came over to me. 'Hi Maggie, I'm sure that first take of the tackle was good, but let's make him work for his money, shall we?' he said with a smile. 'Let's do another twenty tackles.' Happy days. We were surrounded by all the Maidenhead lads who kept cheering me on. 'Come on Maggie, you gotta hit him hard, let's take him down!'

There were definitely a few of the tackles when I put my shoulder into them, and I could hear him grunt when I made contact. I felt bad because tackling was my 'superpower' and should only be used in a safe place, on the rugby pitch. I genuinely didn't want to hurt him with a 'Maggie tackle'.

Eventually Jack had, not surprisingly, had enough. 'Can we stop now? I'm not really enjoying this,' he said. To be fair, he took his tackles and was great company. He was a rising star at that stage but was really down to earth, and almost came across as shy, despite his brilliantly dry wit. And I loved being back in the rugby environment, even if it was only for four days of filming. And a lot less stressful than pretending to be a soprano!

TWENTY

THE LONG SHOT

My first sporting hero wasn't a rugby player. As I've already explained, no one from my council estate was interested in rugby back then. It was Spurs or Arsenal. If you weren't into football, then the other kids wanted to represent Great Britain at the Olympics Games.

Even when I'd return to the area many years later as a world champion, visiting schools with my winners' medal around my neck, they would ask: 'Is that an Olympic medal?' They just couldn't understand what a Rugby World Cup medal was.

I'd tell them: 'It's like an Olympic gold medal but in rugby. A Rugby World Cup comes around every four years, just like the Olympics.' More often than not the faces would be blank. The only currency is football or the Olympics, that is the mindset.

I was exactly the same as a kid. I wasn't really into football. My hero was Denise Lewis.

There was something about her that resonated with me, beyond her remarkable sporting prowess as one of Britain's finest-ever track and field athletes. She had been born in West Bromwich and raised in a single-parent family. Both parents were Jamaican-born but her father left the family home before she had been born, just like mine had. The unconventional upbringing didn't define her, and she was determined to make the most of her sporting talent, and by the age of fifteen was taking two buses and a train journey after school to training for the most gruelling endurance event in women's track and field: the heptathlon.

Her story resonated with me so strongly as it was just as I was beginning my journey with rugby that I became engrossed in the Olympic Games in Atlanta in 1996, where she was a rare British success, winning a bronze medal. I was absolutely hooked. I'd watched the 1995 Rugby World Cup in South Africa, which was fantastic, but this was different. It seemed to bring together elite sport, music and entertainment. Four years later, in Sydney, Denise won gold. Her legacy would be far-reaching. Over 10,000 miles away in Edmonton, I was left with a burning ambition to take part in the Olympics one day.

It was an ambition that, despite everything I'd achieved with rugby, refused to fade. And so, with my England career over, and the pre-World Cup warning from my knee surgeon that I only had a year left of rugby, in a moment that some people might regard as madness, I decided to give it a go.

I wanted to see out the season with Saracens and it meant so much to me that we concluded the campaign as league and English cup champions, even if my final club match was played in front of a handful of spectators, a reminder of just how far the women's game had yet to travel, despite our national status as champions of the world.

My knee may have run out of miles, but I still felt physically strong and fit. I remember thinking: *I still have something to give to elite sport.* I was only thirty-one and still wanted to do something that would give me the same emotional highs that I'd experienced by winning the World Cup. I only had to look around me to see others attempting to make major transitions. Sam Burgess, the rugby league legend, had signed for Bath, switching codes to rugby union in order to pursue his dream of playing for England in the 2015 World Cup. Sonny Bill Williams, the New Zealand phenomenon, had gone even further, switching from rugby league to boxing to rugby union.

My options were more limited, given my knee issues but, one night, as I tossed and turned wondering what to do, my childhood dreams returned: athletics. Why couldn't I have a shot at following the footsteps of my hero Denise by attempting to qualify for the Olympic Games in Rio? Or even Tokyo in 2020?

I'd excelled in throwing events as a child: javelin, discus . . . and shot put. Of the three, shot put had always been my favourite discipline. My passion for athletics sparked during a school trip to the Queen Elizabeth Stadium in Enfield for a training session. During the visit we got to meet Steve Backley, the Great Britain javelin thrower who held the world record and would go on to win Olympic silver medals in the Atlanta and Sydney Games, having won a bronze in Barcelona in 1992. He was a larger-than-life character, a giant of a man with golden hair. I was a small black girl and most of our class were from ethnic minority backgrounds. I didn't have a clue who this big man was. He introduced himself and we all asked him to sign our school journals, even though we told him that we'd have to google him when we got home.

I look back now and laugh at my ignorance. But he still had an impact. When I next went down to the track, this time without the school, I inquired about throwing the javelin and soon hooked up with a coach, who turned out to be the husband of one of my teachers, Mrs Waugh. She was a drama teacher who had a senior leadership role in the school. She also was one of the many teachers who helped keep me on track during my rebel days. Her husband was a mature man who wore a baseball cap and had an athletic build.

The connections and first touchpoints with athletics enhanced the feeling that this sport was my destiny. I was being coached by the husband of one my teachers, I'd met Steve Backley and thought he was really cool, and the Queen Elizabeth Stadium was much closer to home – it was still a bus ride away, but way closer to home than the rugby grounds.

I also had a discus coach called Richard. He always reminded me of a typical PE teacher you would see in the old movies – he'd wear a silvery blue all-in-one tracksuit and glasses and he was in his sixties. He was a lovely man, a volunteer who took me under his wing, introduced me to using the gym and handling weights. He believed in me and my capabilities and felt I could have gone far in the sport if I'd stuck with it. My abiding memory is his commitment to the sport. It's what I loved about athletics: there were so many volunteers, helping people improve not for money but for the love of the sport. It's a passion that is reflected through grassroots rugby clubs across the country.

When I left rugby, it was a passion that I wanted to reconnect with through athletics. Like rugby, it is a sport that shines a light on your core strengths. If you can run fast, you are a sprinter; if you are strong and powerful, you can be a thrower. That was good enough for me.

The London Games in 2012 also touched me while I was still playing for England. The biggest sports show in the world came to my hometown! The Olympic Park was practically a stone's throw away from Edmonton. A fifteen-minute drive down the A406 and then the A12 takes you straight to Stratford. At that time, all the main athletes who were based in north London trained at Lee Valley athletics centre, where I would train when I was playing for England. So I got to meet stars like Christine Ohuruogu, the 400-metre runner, and became good friends with her. Adam Gemilli, one of our top sprinters, was another, while seeing their coaches first-hand also inspired me to think that I could follow in their footsteps.

I would have applied to be a volunteer at the Games but at the time I was hobbling around on crutches because of my knee injury. So, like everyone else in the country, I scrambled to get tickets and, although I missed out on the track and field events, I was still thrilled to go to see the weightlifting and judo at the ExCeL stadium. Well, I say that, but to be honest the judo was a bit of a disappointment as my seat had a restricted view. It got worse. There were also two mats in the arena and the day I was there all the action took place on the other mat right at the far side. I literally couldn't see anything, which was a real shame because I like judo. I guess sometimes these things are better on television!

****

At the time, there were not that many elite women shot putters in the UK. My strength and conditioning training for international rugby meant that I was already in good shape physically. The key was whether there was enough time to learn the throwing technique and mental discipline to get myself into a position to be able to challenge the world's best.

I knew I had a mountain to climb, transitioning to another elite sport that required hours and hours of training as well as innate sporting attributes. But I needed a fresh target, mentally if nothing else, to fill the huge hole in my life left by the end of my rugby career. It is a common challenge for sportspeople to find a new meaning and direction to their lives – often in their mid-thirties, when the all-consuming passion that often began in early childhood comes to an abrupt end.

Yet there was more to it. I also knew I had a responsibility as a female from an ethnic minority background to provide visible leadership to other girls and boys while I still had the athletic ability to do so. When I was engrossed in playing for England, I never thought I was a female playing a male sport, despite the obvious discrepancy between the funding, facilities, opportunities and profile. Nor the fact that for the majority of the time I was often the only black person in our England team. Yet in my role with first the RFU and then the Youth Sport Trust, visiting schools and meeting pupils with ability and energy but not necessarily with the opportunity, it struck me how, even subtly, my participation was opening their eyes to what was possible.

I hope that they looked at me and thought, just as I had drawn inspiration from Denise Lewis: here is someone who came from a black single-parent family, who grew up on a rough council estate in Edmonton and was still able to become a world champion. Every time I heard one of the kids say to me: 'I really want to give rugby a go,' it made everything worthwhile. I can remember meeting a girl from a religious background who loved touch rugby and played in a veil.

I felt it was also important to show girls who may be body conscious that they could be proud of how they looked. I can remember as a teenager thinking that my thighs were really big. I also had big arms. But it was my physique that allowed me to be a successful sportsperson. I think a number of our sporting stars have shown girls that 'sporty is beauty as well' – Jessica Ennis-Hill and Christine Ohuruogu in athletics, Alex Scott and Kelly Smith in football and Rebecca Adlington in swimming. A quote I live by is: 'Life is measured by the impact you have on other people'. Impact is infectious. One person can have a positive impact on a thousand people. That's a legacy.

****

When I retired from rugby, I was 5ft 3in and around 73kg. If I felt I was powerful, I only had to look at the stats of the reigning Olympic and world shot put champion, Val Adams, for a reminder of the standard of competition I would face. At the time she was 6ft 4ins and weighed 120kg – an imposing frame that would compare favourably with a male second row forward. *I literally could have been her shot put!*

They were not the only critical measurements. The shot – a metal sphere – weighs four kilograms for female athletes, nine times the weight of a rugby ball. It takes a huge amount of explosive power and technique to propel it the kind of distances required to be competitive.

When I started throwing again, my early personal best was 11.44m, which was recorded at the Lee Valley stadium where I started my training. It gave me a ranking of forty-third in the country. My target to qualify for Rio was 17.80m. And Val Adams' record? Well, the New Zealander's personal best was 21.24m! Time and distance were against me. But I was determined to give it a go. My target was to have thrown 15 metres by the end of the summer.

I wanted my transition to track and field to be a statement, for others but also for myself. So I decided to make my decision public to pursue my Olympic dream. It would hold me to account too; there was no backing down now.

My first job was to assemble a new team around me. I was no longer a key member of Gary Street's England high-performance squad. I went from being in this really organised and structured set-up with five or six coaches supporting my development as well as a strength and conditioning team to nothing.

The stark reality was I was an athletic nobody who had once shown some level of promising competence when I was a teenager. I was effectively basing my ambition on how to progress up the pathway on what I knew from the past, but that was almost twenty years ago.

The first task was to find myself a coach. It wasn't as easy as it sounds. There was no real structure to coaching in a fashion similar to rugby union. Coaches were attached to athletic stadiums. Some took groups, while other athletes had worked with the same coach since they were a child.

The club that I'd been part of when I was a teenager was Enfield Harriers, which was based at the Queen Elizabeth Stadium in Enfield. My first reaction was that I should go back there, because it was where I first started my athletics journey. So that's what I did. When my story became public, however, it was regarded as quite big sports news: *England's World Cup-winning star sets her sights on Olympic dream.*

It wasn't long before I found myself being 'headhunted'. I was approached by the athletics club that is based at Saracens' StoneX Stadium, Shaftesbury Barnet Harriers, but my loyalties were with Enfield Harriers.

As it turned out, I ended up not training at the Queen Elizabeth Stadium, but at the Lee Valley stadium in Edmonton, but I was still affiliated to Enfield Harriers. Most athletes tended to either train where their coaches were based or where their clubs were, but I trained at the stadium that was close to me and my coach would travel to meet me. Enfield Harriers would then tell me when the next 'meet' was and I would turn up wearing my half red and half yellow club top. It was a different world to what I was used to.

I don't really remember how I found my coach. She was recommended to me because she had worked with a variety of athletes, young and old. She took me under her wing and I saw her twice a week. We started right at the bottom, working on all the basic techniques to get them right first. The main struggle that I had through the whole experience was the one-on-one coaching. It was just me and her. I'd never experienced that before. In rugby, if you fell out with one coach, there was always somebody else to talk to. You were also surrounded by teammates. But this was completely different. It was just the two of us, twice a week. The strain on the relationship was exacerbated by the need to do pretty much the same thing again and again. There were some variations. I would go to the gym to do strength and power work centred around Olympic lifting, but other than that it was repetitive work in the shot-put ring at Lee Valley athletics centre.

The relationship between the coach and athlete also *felt* very different to rugby. It was almost as if the athlete belonged to the coach. In rugby, going through the age groups, you would work with one coach and then move on to the next one at a different level. At the very top of the pyramid, with England, there were a number of coaches to work with and there was a feeling of mutual respect. We trusted them to develop us and frame a game plan, and we would put our heart and soul into training and matches. There are many examples in athletics where the coach takes the athlete from a young age right through the entire journey of their career. I struggled with that concept of 'ownership'. I wanted to see different coaches to develop my technique and conditioning. But I was aligned with the same one and it just became too intense.

I reached out to another coach, a former Great Britain shot putter called Shaun Pickering, son of the late BBC athletics commentator Ron. At the time he was coaching at Loughborough. I was already spending half my week there through my work with the Youth Sport Trust. Most of the Great Britain coaches were based at Loughborough and I was using the gym there called 'Powerbase' and was able to maintain the connections and support from the strength and conditioning coaches there I had used during my rugby days. But it was the technical side that I was struggling with. Shaun was eager to help.

'Come over and I'll have a look,' he said. It was so interesting to hear a different perspective. And eye-opening. 'You don't do that, Maggie,' he said. 'Nor that.' *What?* He ended up not only breaking down my technique, but he also broke me.

I loved his knowledge and understanding. He had also represented Wales and Great Britain in the discus and hammer. He took me under his wing, like a consultant. I was so sad to hear of his passing in May 2023 at the age of just sixty-one. He was a gentle giant who was willing to give up his time for free to help me with my development. I will be forever grateful to him.

I continued to work with my other coach too and, although the joint approach helped, the lack of structure to the year didn't help me.

I was used to working towards dates. Play well for Saracens and you would be named in the England elite-player squad. Then the Six Nations or World Cup squads would be selected. With my big step into the unknown with athletics, I struggled to know what fixed points in the year I was working towards. The only date that seemed to be certain was the start of the Olympic Games in Rio. The only clarity I had was that unless I made it into the GB pathway within the year, I wasn't going to make it. I wasn't making it.

My throwing improved but I didn't get much beyond 12 metres. I needed to be throwing further than this for Enfield to progress. If I didn't feel like I had the right team around me, there was also a growing realisation that I just wasn't good enough. At various points in my rugby career, my teammates may have described me as cocky. I was a confident player. But I also felt I had honesty too. I'd accepted that I wasn't going to make it as a centre because of my distribution skills. I'd adapted to the back row to make best use of my pace and power while working on the weaker parts of my game. But with the shot put, the gap was just too wide to bridge. I was running out of time and the years were also against me.

The challenge now was to decide my next step. I'd made a big statement about pursuing my Olympic dream, but I was the only one who knew it would now remain a fanciful hope.

I had only pushed it into the public domain in order to get the right support. That had taken me so far. No one from UK Sport had been in touch with me, and understandably so. They must be inundated with people declaring their ambition to be Olympians.

Yet there was part of me left wondering what I could have achieved with the right support. Look at Victoria Pendleton, who made the transition from cycling to horse racing with the support of a betting company. She achieved her goal and now loves working with horses. I also knew several Paralympians who had transitioned into other sports successfully, so I knew it was possible.

I felt like I had the qualities and the mindset and the attitudes and the skill, but not necessarily the right support. And maybe that's because I didn't get the right team around me to give me that support.

I guess people were right to see my ambition to represent Great Britain at the Olympics as delusional. I underestimated the task of building a new team around me, despite the positive influence of people like Shaun. The pathway that I experienced as a teenager just wasn't there. I'd started out right on the bottom rung and hoped to climb to the top of the ladder in months, not years.

At the end of my rugby career, I just didn't have the energy and the time to commit to forging the right relationships, understanding the pathway and finding the right coaches.

The biggest dream of my sporting career had ended up in my biggest failure. Rather than make a song and dance about it, I just slipped away. There was no point making another big announcement because I had nothing to announce.

Yet I look back with no regrets. I put myself out there and tried to realise the dream that I had as a young girl. And by putting myself out there, it would open new doors for me that

I could never have imagined. Out of the blue I received a text message from a senior member of staff at ITV asking if I wanted to be part of the broadcast team for the 2015 Rugby World Cup in England. It hadn't yet been a year since my tearful England retirement but a whole new rugby journey was about to begin.

TWENTY-ONE

OWNING MY VOICE

The world in front of me was rapidly changing. New opportunities brought new challenges too. On the rugby pitch I may have had doubts at times, but if I did, they were linked to performance. I knew what I could do and, in my best form, I knew I had the physical prowess and athleticism that few players in the world could match.

Yet there was no playbook for transitioning from international player to the next phase of my life. What had driven me on were two fundamentals – the desire to set myself new goals, which I'd already been thinking about back in my hotel room the night that we had won the World Cup, and taking myself out of my comfort zone. That had initially been rugby, but for over a decade playing in the back row for club and country had been my safe place. I knew it was where I could express myself, my talent and my strengths.

Taking part in the Children in Need choir, featuring in a television commercial with Jack Whitehall and trying but ultimately failing to become an Olympic shot putter had been challenging, fun and fulfilling adventures in different ways. And I guess each represented small but important steps forward to opening up the biggest opportunity, responsibility and challenge in my post-playing career: the world of broadcasting.

I'd already done bits and pieces of media work before the contact came in the summer of 2015 from ITV asking if I would consider being part of their broadcasting team for the men's World Cup in England.

In 2013, when I was recovering from my knee injury, I was a pundit for Sky Sports covering England women's three-Test tour in New Zealand. I found it tough, really tough. We lost all three Tests, and I found myself in an impossible place. I was still a player, and my loyalty was to my teammates. Imagine being in that position and having to criticise your mates live on television. But what I know now is that as a broadcaster you cannot sit on the fence. I learned the hard way during those two weeks. I learned not to say 'we' when talking about England, because I was there to talk objectively about England or New Zealand.

Sky Sports were great, however, and I have always had a lot of time for them because they were the first broadcaster to take women's rugby seriously. They covered our World Cup finals in 2006, 2010 and 2014, with increasing coverage of the tournament.

There had been other broadcasting touching points with Sky as a pundit. One of my early highlights was appearing on their old *Rugby Club* show, hosted by Alex Payne and featuring Will Greenwood, Dewi Morris and Stuart Barnes. It was a great show, dealing with the issues of the week and previewing the weekend's matches. I was on to talk about the old Tri Nations, now known as the Rugby Championship. I knew my rugby, I watched a lot of games, but couldn't help feeling incredibly nervous going on to the show and relaying my insights. Stuart Barnes was fantastic. 'Maggie, don't overthink it, just say what you know,' he said. I loved that. I also did some work experience at Sky Sports News and it opened my eyes. I saw all the action in front and behind the cameras. I observed the news readers, sat in meetings with key influencers at the business, I immersed myself in the gallery and studied the production team. It was insightful and interesting and I came away with a thirst for more. The most powerful thing I witnessed was seeing the news readers occasionally make mistakes live on air and, if they did, seeing that it wasn't the end of the world. They just continued on and wasted no time dwelling on it. It's what I feared: making mistakes. But after seeing the professionals at work, I realised they were human too.

As a player, I was sometimes asked to do an extended interview by the BBC during half-time of an England men's match at Twickenham to give a quick preview of our Test match that we would be playing afterwards at the same stadium. If I'd enjoyed those moments, I knew the offer to work with the ITV team at the men's World Cup would be completely different. There were those doubts again – far, far worse than anything I had experienced as a player. Could I really do this?

One dictionary definition of 'imposter syndrome' describes it as: 'Anxiety or self-doubt that results from persistently undervaluing one's competence and active role in achieving success, while falsely attributing one's accomplishments to luck or other external forces.'

I'd won a World Cup with England, played in two other World Cup finals, had won seventy-four caps for my country and scored twenty-eight tries. I'd played in an England team that had won a record-breaking seven successive Six Nations titles. I had an MBE for service to rugby. But I was a woman being asked to give her opinion live on television on the men's World Cup, the third-biggest global sporting event behind the Olympics and the football World Cup. And I was the first woman to be asked to do that in men's teams sport in this country. I wondered if I was worthy enough. What would people think of me, a female player most people had not heard of, trying to give my opinion on the men's game? I don't think I've ever been racked with a more overwhelming feeling of insecurity at any other time in my life.

I was being asked to work alongside some of the biggest names from the men's game: Sir Clive Woodward, Jonny Wilkinson, Lawrence Dallaglio, Brian O'Driscoll, George Gregan, Sir Ian McGeechan, Francois Pienaar, Sean Fitzpatrick and Michael Lynagh. And the girl from a council estate in Edmonton Green.

Some trailblazing women had worked in rugby broadcasting as reporters and presenters for years, such as Sonja McLaughlan, Jill Douglas, Sara Orchard and Gabby Logan. Mary Nightingale, the brilliant ITV news presenter, also worked on the 1991 and 1995 World Cups. Thankfully, we're now used to seeing lots of female faces employed as pundits in men's and women's sport, such as Alex Scott in football, Ebony Rainford-Brent in cricket and the list goes on.

But before 2015, no female former rugby player had ever commentated on the men's game before. And nothing could prepare me for the vitriol of sexist comments that would follow my decision to join the ITV team. It was time to don the tin hat. But first, more importantly, I had to find my voice and own it.

****

People might be surprised to learn that I grew up with a stammer. I don't think it was ever classified as an official stammer, but I've always had difficulty pronouncing certain words and frequently stumble when speaking. If I was asked to read a passage from a book during an English class at school, my levels of anxiety would shoot up if it contained a word that I knew I would struggle with, embarrassed that I'd make a fool of myself. I've always spoken very quickly (at least, people have told me that I do), at times too quickly, causing me to stutter over my words. My thinking at the time was: the sooner I got it done, the sooner the focus will be off me. When I spoke fast, I could see in people's faces that they didn't understand what I was saying. It was frustrating.

My appearances when I was coming to the end of my playing career allowed me to serve an apprenticeship. I tried to learn from my mistakes and took in advice like a sponge. I watched Stuart Barnes, Dewi Morris and Will Greenwood on the *Rugby Club*. I was a big fan of watching Will – he was a character, an entertainer and understood production. Broadcasting evolved too, from being largely studio-based to more pitch-side reporting and analysis.

But when the offer came from ITV, I wanted – and needed – more than bit-part experience. So, I signed up for a broadcasting course in London. Everyone on the course wanted to be a broadcaster or TV presenter. It was fascinating. We went through everything – I learned how to use an earpiece, read autocue, how to speak when someone was talking in my ear, how to put showreels together and work camera angles. It was like a crash course in broadcasting and production. Not everyone will need to do it, but I felt it was necessary. It is one thing knowing your sport; knowing how to be a media professional is very different.

I had a brief chat with Mary Nightingale to pick her brains on what it was like reporting on the two World Cups as a woman. 'It was challenging,' she admitted. She'd been a reporter and presenter, which was a challenge in itself. But I was going to have to give my opinion and analysis.

ITV sent us a list of the games I would be covering around four weeks in advance. I started writing wads of notes about each game. I wrote so much that it became like a series of dissertations. It's something I still do before every game – I might as well be the commentator, as I write down pages of notes on each player as well!

One of the things I've always prided myself on is my preparation, but I would quickly learn the best methods are not always orthodox. One of the pool games I was assigned to involved Georgia. My research set alarm bells ringing. Reading through the names of the players, I realised that I'd struggle to pronounce any of them. I could feel the terror from my English class return many times over. The one thing you cannot do as a broadcaster is pronounce names incorrectly.

I phoned an old friend, Simon Ward, who is a hugely experienced broadcaster who had commentated on many of our England and Saracens matches. He was also working for ITV on the World Cup.

'Simon, please help!' I pleaded. 'I've been put down to do one of the Georgia games and I can't say any of their names. Can we meet up?'

Simon was based in Hertfordshire, so we met up at South Mimms service station. 'Don't worry,' he said, 'I'll help you go through the names.'

We sat down at a table in one of the cafes, Simon started reading out the names, but he was struggling a bit with the pronunciations as well. I was starting to panic again. Then, a lady who was cleaning the table next to us, came over.

'Hello, I am sorry to interrupt, but I am from Georgia, I can help you with the names,' she said, like an angel from heaven. What were the chances? But that is exactly what she did and by the end I was just about confident enough that I would be able to get through the match.

If I'd done my best to prepare for this opportunity, my first game at the Rugby World Cup was still an eye-opener. France versus Romania at the Queen Elizabeth Olympic Park. At least it wasn't far from home. Another big black Mercedes came to pick me up, once again raising eyebrows on the estate. My last visit to the stadium had been three years earlier, taking the train as a spectator on my crutches to watch the Paralympics.

We met the production team three hours before kick-off, and, despite all my preparation, I still remember being racked with nerves. There were portacabins set up for the broadcasting teams and one of the first people I met was Craig Doyle, who I'd only really seen before from the double-glazing adverts. What you see is what you get with Craig. A lovely Irishman, who is so warm and friendly. I guess he knew I was a bit nervous, but he said: 'Just relax Maggie and enjoy it. I'll talk you through everything and just go with the flow.'

The next person I bumped into was the All Blacks legend Sean Fitzpatrick. I was struck by how relaxed he was. He had a huge standing in the game and was also an experienced broadcaster. Seeing how Craig and Sean were had a calming effect on me. 'Treat it as if you're talking about the game with your mate in the pub,' they told me. We talked through which person was going to cover what aspect of the game in the pre-match chat. And I learned a lesson from Sean about dealing with the dreaded moment when you might struggle with pronunciation or remembering a player's name. He just paused, put his glasses on and unravelled the team sheet and read it out smoothly and with authority. It was another moment that made me feel more at ease. If you make a mistake, you move on without breaking your stride.

After the show I received a lovely text message from Mark Demuth, ITV's controller of sport, saying: 'Well done, Maggie, you looked really relaxed and enjoyed it.' It was reassuring to hear. *Wow, I just did it.* I got on with it, made mistakes, tried to learn from them. My last game was the third/fourth play-off between South Africa and Argentina, when I was working with Bryan Habana. It was a sprint to the finish line, and I finished the tournament feeling like I had evolved into a rugby pundit and wanted more.

From my time in rugby and, briefly, in athletics, I realised the importance of getting a good team around me. I hired Gavin Scovell, who trains presenters and was one of the directors for ITV during the tournament. He became a mentor for me over the next few years, giving me feedback so that I could work on and improve my delivery. I also hired a voice coach and had elocution lessons to improve the clarity in my voice. I appreciated the importance of being able to communicate clearly and be understood, especially as I used to stumble over my words when I spoke too fast. He worked with me to slow down the pace of my speech and make it more authoritative. I now work with Rob Nothman, the BBC sports broadcaster and producer who has trained almost everyone who joins the BBC, and Matt Curtis, a sports TV producer, broadcast coach and media consultant. Before every rugby match I work with them to prepare for a show, and review the shows with them afterwards. I receive critical feedback (good and bad), which I digest and then action, and I'm still on that journey. I don't believe anyone is perfect, but the key is to strive to be the best version of yourself and never stop learning. I had the same attitude when I was an England player (and a shot putter!). I surround myself with people who would help me realise my potential. I created my 'Team Maggie'. I actively identified people who were specialists in their field to work with and I utilised their feedback and expertise to grow.

Presenting skills, however, are only half the battle. I didn't notice many negative comments about my performances during the World Cup, but it didn't take long for the vitriol to start pouring in when I was asked back to work during the men's Six Nations Championship. I'd started to take more of an interest in the reaction on social media, in my ignorance looking for positive feedback.

For my first game I was in Dublin for England's match against Ireland. I was pitchside with Martin Bayfield, who at 6ft 10ins is almost a foot and a half taller than me. He towered over me. The comments on social media started off seemingly harmless enough. 'It must be "bring your daughter to work" day,' wrote one. 'Why is there a woman talking about rugby?' 'What does she know about rugby?' But it would get much, much worse.

I was alongside the former Ireland and Lions centre Gordon D'Arcy and felt the confidence evaporate. But going into my shell was the worst thing I could have done.

My voice became even more muted when I was in Rome for Italy's match against England. It was the first time I was in the studio for a match and was joined by Sir Clive Woodward, Jonny Wilkinson and the presenter, Mark Poutgach. All I could think was: 'Oh my God! Jonny Wilkinson kicked the drop-goal to win the World Cup for England and Sir Clive was head coach of the side. They're both rugby gods.' I felt so proud. Mum couldn't believe her girl was on TV. I still have a photograph of us all in the studio that afternoon on my Twitter profile.

But as we went live, my head was filled with thoughts of angry viewers typing on their phones to post abuse on social media, and it heightened my own insecurity. *What on earth could I say to add value to the punditry, sitting beside these two rugby giants?* My World Cup win felt insignificant to what the 2003 men's team had achieved, even though I'd worked so hard for eleven years to lift the trophy. It might have been wrong to think that way, but it was how I felt at the time. If you needed a description of a shrinking violet, that was me that afternoon in Rome. Every time Jonny spoke, I agreed. Every time Sir Clive spoke, I agreed. How was I going to disagree with those two? I wasn't helped by the format. First question to Jonny, second question to Sir Clive. I was wondering what question I'd be left with. I was trying to add to the analysis but felt I was just repeating what the other two had said. It was a chastening experience. I reviewed my performance over and over again. I felt that I'd been trying to say things that would please people in the studio and the viewers. When the lights went on, the camera started rolling and the countdown to us going on air started, it sapped my personality and opinions. During the World Cup, when I had no expectations, I had found it much easier to be myself.

During the Six Nations, it was different. I became increasingly aware of the pressure of being the only woman involved as a pundit. I can remember Alex Scott tweeting during the championship, saying something like how awesome it was to see me in the studio working on the men's Six Nations and I hope football follows suit. She was still playing for Arsenal then.

There were plenty of supportive voices like hers, and I had a responsibility not to let people down. Conversely, in a way the pressure made it harder to find my voice and express my own personality.

But I knew there could be no going back. If I failed, it would only make it harder for those who would follow me. Rightly or wrongly, at that moment I was the most high-profile player in England. It has been brilliant to see the likes of my old rehab buddy Nolli Waterman, Philippa Tuttiett, Emily Scarratt, Rocky Clarke, Kat Merchant, Rachel Burford, Katy Daley-Mclean and Mo Hunt doing media work in recent years. More are following and as it becomes the norm for women to be pundits in sport – in men's and women's sport – so the spotlight on their performance purely on gender will fade away. But in 2016, I felt everyone was watching me. If I wanted to be a visible leader, I had to ditch the imposter syndrome and step out of the shadows of the men that I was working alongside.

I'd won a World Cup of my own. My opinion had value and weight. I didn't have to agree with fellow pundits, even if I was in awe of what they'd achieved in the game. It doesn't matter if I'm a woman. A black woman. It's about being able to deliver. I've always worked hard throughout my life. I took part-time jobs when I was at school and as a student to help my mum with the household finances. I wasn't arrogant enough to assume that all I had to do was turn up and spout off the first thing that came into my head. Before each game I was prepared. I thought I knew my stuff. I knew that would never be enough for some people, who would judge me for the colour of my skin or my gender or sexuality. But I know now in the first few appearances I'd not helped myself but not *being* myself. I'd lost my personality, I wasn't being my authentic self and as a result I'd lost my voice.

I went to see Mark Demuth and Phil Heslop, the programme editor at ITV Sport. They were both brilliant in helping me. Mark said, 'Maggie, we're a broadcaster, not a narrowcaster. Be broad, entertain. ITV is free to view so invite new viewers to watch rugby by the way you are. Don't just aim to please rugby people. Imagine that your mum's watching. Broaden people's horizons and entertain by showing your personality.' Those words still sit with me today. It was such a lovely way to look at it. I watched others. David Flatman has fantastic rugby knowledge but wraps it up with humour. That may not work for everyone, but it's entertaining. Gareth Thomas, the former Wales and Lions captain, is another who always passionately tries to be himself.

'Be authentic, that's what people want to see,' Mark added.

****

So I found my voice again. At times I can tell when I feel I'm losing it again and Mark's words spur me on. I still make mistakes, but who doesn't? I'm still learning, but nowadays I'm not trying to be someone else or please people I think I should please.

I have loved being part of the ITV rugby family. Everyone is so supportive and when we're away on trips your colleagues become like an extended family.

Becoming part of the rugby media family has taken me places I could only have dreamed of. Like many former players, making the transition hasn't been easy, particularly when I'm working in the women's game and still know some of the players involved. But you have to approach it in a professional manner. Bumping into players and coaches after matches can, at times, be awkward, especially if they've had a bad game and you've had to criticise their performance on air.

The morning after England men had lost the 2019 World Cup final to South Africa in Yokohama sticks out. I was standing waiting for the lift in my hotel in Tokyo to go to the gym for my routine workout. When the lift doors opened, there was Eddie Jones, the England head coach. Our hotel was beside the one that the England squad had been staying in and they had used the pool in our hotel for recovery sessions. Eddie and some of his staff had also been using our gym. I stepped into the lift. We acknowledged each other with a nod of the head and a tentative smile.

The dreadful lift music was humming in the background. I didn't know what to do. This was the same Eddie Jones who'd seen me tackle Owen Farrell a lifetime ago. The previous evening, I'd been a pundit covering his side's crushing defeat by the Springboks. I knew the pain of losing a World Cup final, twice. Now Eddie had lost two himself as a head coach, having also lost to England when he was in charge of Australia in 2003. I'd seen him on the cross-trainer quite often in our gym during the previous two weeks. But what could I say to kill those awkward seconds?

Congratulating him on reaching the final didn't seem appropriate. I know he didn't want to talk about the final and hear my commiserations either, but I couldn't say *nothing*. So I said, 'I'm sorry,' and he kindly acknowledged me and the rest of the moment passed in silence, probably the first time both of us were lost for words.

****

Sadly, the abuse on social media didn't stop. In 2020, following the murder of George Floyd in America and the Black Lives Matter protests, the RFU announced it would be reviewing the singing of 'Swing Low, Sweet Chariot' at Twickenham because of its slavery origin. I did an interview with Sky Sports to explain why I would no longer sing the song. The racist abuse I received was astonishing.

I almost always ignore it, but it got so bad that I fired back. I was born in London, I'm English through and through, I had given blood, sweat and tears to represent my country with pride. I'd won a World Cup for my country. And yet some people were telling me, among other things, to 'f*** off back home'.

I posted my own message: 'Thank you @SkySports for conducting this interview with me to discuss the Swing Low, Sweet Chariot song and the RFU review into it. The comments below the piece say it all. It demonstrates exactly why I will NEVER stop using my voice!!'

I scrolled through the replies to find the worst of the racist abuse and took a screenshot. I still have it. Every day when doubts resurface or I feel like I'm losing my voice again, I look at it to remind myself of why I have to keep going. Why I'm never going to give up the fight. It makes me smile that those people who direct abuse at me are in the process making me more determined.

In the first game of the 2021 Six Nations, Italy faced France in Rome. I was in the studio with Gareth Thomas, and Jill Douglas was the main presenter, while Nolli was commentating with Miles Harrison. It appeared that having three women working at the same match proved too much for some.

Nolli had been subjected to horrendous abuse after working at a match the previous autumn. This was a woman who had won seven Six Nations titles, played in three World Cup finals, winning the last, and won eighty-two caps for England. I had first-hand experience of sitting with her for weeks, sometimes months, rehabbing together from injuries when the easier option would have been to quit. But this apparently wasn't enough for the trolls.

When they went after all three of us during the Italy game, I decided to respond again. First on Twitter and then in my column with the *Daily Telegraph* newspaper.

'A good afternoon in the studio for ITAvFRA,' I wrote on Twitter. 'As expected though, many sexist comments about women working on men's rugby. Those who comment are not worthy of a response. Rugby is not a gender; it's a sport and my accolades far outweigh what any of those sexist individuals have achieved!!

'Thank you to those who have shown their support. It's been overwhelming. For those who continue to comment on my gender, I say, mine (and many other women's voices) will never be silenced regardless of how hard they try to oppress it. Thanks to ITV for your continued support too.'

I developed the point in my *Telegraph* column. 'I sometimes wonder about the source of sexist comments, and whether it is insecurity or to do with people's upbringing,' I wrote. 'A lot of responses suggested the sexists were not real rugby fans, which might be true. They are probably trolls who try to get a kick out of trying to make someone feel bad.

'Well, that is not going to work with me. The support I received after my post was staggering – and it came from men and women. I really appreciated Gareth Thomas's message. It is more about being championed by a rugby expert – again, regardless of gender. We are in this together.

'There are women all around this Six Nations, with presenters such as Gabby Logan, Sonja McLaughlan, Sara Orchard and

Jill Douglas. Former Ireland international Joy Neville was the television match official for Scotland's win over England. They are all doing an awesome job and have to do so while putting up with regular abuse. A shout-out to them. I hope my voice here, and the platform I have to use it, will go some way to eventually silencing these keyboard warriors.'

Those words still ring true. One day I hope that a person's gender, race or sexuality will no longer be held against them. What I've discovered with broadcasting is that it exposes you to both the best and worst of society. It was rare for me to experience any of these negative comments. But once you are on the TV giving your opinions, it seems you're fair game.

I'm good friends with Alex Scott now, and many other female broadcasters, and together we're shifting the dial. I now see more women within media and in journalism. It feels great to be part of what feels like a game-changing generation. To have been part of that journey, even if it has just been a small part, makes enduring all the abuse seem worthwhile. The quote by Mahatma Gandhi perfectly sums it up: 'Be the change you wish to see in the world.'

TWENTY-TWO

MY GREATEST ACHIEVEMENT

Bumping into Eddie Jones in a lift wasn't my highlight of the 2019 Rugby World Cup. Neither was watching his England side tear apart New Zealand in an extraordinary semi-final performance.

No, my standout moment in Japan came just a few days before that epic encounter in Yokohama, when Marcella, my partner, asked me to marry her with a surprise proposal. I had a day off and Marcella said she'd booked a couple of trips. 'Great, it'll be nice to see a bit more of Tokyo,' I said.

What I didn't know was the level of planning that had gone into these 'trips' – and how a glance at my ITV mobile phone could have completely ruined the surprise.

I'd first met Marcella at Saracens. She was also a back row forward. But, as she often reminds me, I hadn't noticed her when she first joined the club because she started off playing for the 2nd XV. She might have a point there, but I insist differently. (Seriously, Marcella!)

We do laugh about it. Soon afterwards, she was promoted to the first team and switched to the second row because there were so many of us in the back row. She was working as a personal trainer but also working in marketing to help universities recruit students. Alongside being marketing mad, her other passion has been the health and wellbeing of others. From marathons to cross-fit and being a coach at our local rugby club, being active is a big part of who she is and a massive synergy for us as a couple. She was always thinking of other people through activities on top of her day job. I think her altruism is one of the things that attracted me to her. We were both driven and passionate people and that alignment brought us together. At least once she'd made the 1st XV! Outside of sport and fitness, we had other similar interests including a love of animals. On our first date, Marcella turned up, dog bed in hand, with her two miniature schnauzers, Muffin and Tinker, and apologised for their muddy paws (to say I'm a bit obsessed with a clean house is an understatement . . .). Since then, we've enjoyed many a walk and cuddle with them on the sofa and we also work with our local animal rescue to volunteer, which is important to us both. We got together during the Six Nations after the men's World Cup because she told me she kept seeing me on the television, with the Samsung adverts and another one I did for 'Visit England' and then working as a pundit. 'I kept seeing you everywhere,' she told me later. 'It was like a sign.'

By the time we travelled to Japan together, we'd talked about marriage, and joked, given that we were in a same-sex relationship, about who might do the asking. Honestly, I always thought it would be me, which is why what happened next was such a surprise. But that was far from my mind when we headed off together to visit a light museum in Tokyo. I must admit, I wasn't in great form. We had to queue for ages to get in and afterwards jumped in a taxi and arrived at what looked like an abandoned warehouse. Marcella turned to me and said she had to run in to check something out first and asked me to wait. 'I've booked us on a helicopter ride.' I have to admit at that moment my heart sank. I wasn't a fan of helicopter rides. A few years earlier, she'd booked one for my birthday. She'd got it through a discount website and when we got there it looked like it was held together by sticky tape and the pilot couldn't start it the first time. I remember thinking: 'Today is the day that I am going to die.' He finally got it going and when we got into the air he asked me to take control of the stick. 'Just keep us on our current course and be soft on the pedals,' said the pilot. I don't know what happened, but we started to lose altitude and he had to grab the stick from me. 'Okay, let's try that again,' said the pilot, once we'd stabilised. But once again when I took over, we went down. 'I don't want to do this anymore,' I told him. The lesson was supposed to last thirty minutes but we were back on the ground in half that time. Ever since then, I've had an issue with helicopter flying. Which explains my lack of enthusiasm for Marcella's booking . . . again!

I looked across at her talking to a man at the front office. She was trying to explain that she was going to propose to me on the flight but she was concerned that the ring she had for me in her pocket would set the alarm off during security. She wanted him to take the ring through security in advance to hide it from me. The problem was that he spoke barely any English, and she didn't speak any Japanese. Looking on from afar, I thought they were having an argument. 'Maybe we won't have to go through with this flight,' I thought to myself, selfishly.

But within a minute the row appeared to be over and Marcella came back to the car. 'We're all good to go,' she said. Oh well.

Unlike the previous flight, when we walked past two cool-looking helicopters to get on the dodgy-looking one, this time we headed towards a sleek black machine, which wasn't much taller than I was. It looked awesome. By the time we took off, darkness had fallen and the flight was beautiful, flying over the lights of Tokyo. I can't lie, I was absolutely terrified, looking at the dazzling and colourful night lights through my fingers.

The pilot turned to us and said something that I couldn't hear. My mind raced back to our previous flight. 'Just fly the thing, would you,' I mouthed back. Marcella turned to me. 'Are you having a great time?' she asked.

'I have to say, it's much more enjoyable than I thought it would be,' I replied.

'Well, it's just about to get a lot better,' she said and produced a beautiful diamond ring. I couldn't believe it. I'd always assumed that I would be the one who was going to propose. It was the best thing ever, absolutely the best thing ever. I said yes, of course, and then the pilot turned to us and asked if we wanted a photograph. He'd been in on it. When we landed, the staff arrived. 'Did she say "yes"?' one asked. I looked at Marcella. '*Everyone* was in on this? I thought you were having an argument at the start!' I said.

Unfortunately, we couldn't get a taxi to come to the warehouse, so we walked along a busy highway to get to a service station to call one. 'Do you want to call your mum?' Marcella asked. Good idea. So, from a service station along a busy highway in Tokyo, I phoned Mum, back in her flat in Edmonton. She was elated. We'd come a long way from those early days when she struggled to come to terms with my sexuality. The 6,000-mile phone call from Tokyo to London was symbolic of the remarkable journey that rugby had taken me on. I hoped it had helped change her life too.

Marcella's meticulous plans for this special day were not yet finished. Secretly, she had informed the ITV rugby team about her intentions and they had organised everyone to assemble at the bar in our hotel to greet us when we returned.

And what a star-studded reception party it was – Brian O'Driscoll, Bryan Habana, Gareth Thomas, Shane Williams, Jill Douglas, Nick Mullins, Nolli Waterman . . . An engagement party to remember! We went into town for drinks and Marcella's final request was for us to go to karaoke. Nolli, Brian and Shane were also up for it. To celebrate our engagement with such fantastic people from the world of rugby made for a special night. A day that had begun as a nondescript day off and turned into one of the greatest days of my life, all thanks to Marcella.

Mercifully, I'd not glanced at my ITV mobile earlier in the day. One of the team members that Marcella had told had put out a group message to organise the engagement party that evening, without remembering that I was on the group too! 'Marcella is going to propose to Maggie today, and this evening we're going to have a massive engagement party,' they wrote. As it was my day off, I hadn't bothered to check my phone. I don't know what I would have done if I'd seen the message. Maybe I would have played along, pretending ignorance so as not to spoil Marcella's surprise. Who knows? I'm just thankful I missed the message. I guess it was meant to be.

****

The following year the world was gripped by the Covid pandemic, and the lockdown gave us time to plan our wedding. I think we changed the date about three times and eventually tied the knot in October 2021, with a reception at the Crazy Bear hotel in Oxford. Although we initially wanted a small wedding, that just wasn't going to happen with our huge rugby family. Marcella used to play at Hampstead Rugby Club before she moved to Saracens, so she had some friends from there. Former teammates from Saracens came too, and a handful of my former England teammates and management were there, such as Catherine Spencer, Tamara Taylor, Hannah Gallagher, Kat Merchant, Nessie Gray, Helen Clayton, Assunta De Biase, Claire Frost, Maxine Edwards, Emma Mitchell, Amy Garnett, Gary Street, Graham Smith and Julia Hutton. Sadly, Nolli and Heather

Fisher couldn't make it. But the PE teacher who changed the course of my life and my first Saracens coach, Liza Burgess and Katie Ball, were both in attendance. Not to mention Marcella's wonderful family, many of whom travelled from Ireland to bring the party. It was the right environment, the right mix of people, the right music and the right level of alcohol in the room.

I couldn't have enjoyed it any more. My one concern had been being in the spotlight all day. I'd been the same on my wonderful, crazy hen night in Bournemouth. I'd been really looking forward to the company, but not the attention. But in reality, having all our close friends in one space, and all the people who've played a big part in our lives, was incredibly moving. We shared stories and laughs, and at one stage ended up with a lineout on the dance floor. On most of my rugby night outs, we'd usually end up with a lineout (I was always the lifter though, it always seemed safer having my feet on the ground). Our journey had started off in rugby, we'd got engaged during the Rugby World Cup, and now were married, surrounded by our rugby friends.

When people ask me about the game, I always tell them that rugby *saved* my life, rugby *changed* my life and rugby has *given* me a life. I will always be forever grateful to the sport for that. I just hope that my children are able to get the same opportunities out of the game that I did.

At the time of writing this book, Marcella and I are also proud parents to two children, Artie and Willow (and to two miniature Schnauzer dogs, Nala and Tinker). Their arrival has changed everything. I can honestly say that whatever achievements I managed on the rugby pitch, or off it since, I regard their arrival as the greatest achievement of all.

I'd always wanted to be a mother but always feared it wasn't going to be possible. Like most people I worried about meeting the right partner but I also had the complexity of my sporting career. Should I try to get pregnant before I started playing for England?

I could get maternity leave through the company I was working for, but there was nothing from the RFU at that stage if you were playing for England. It's great to see the RFU, together with the Rugby Players Association, have negotiated and agreed maternity leave as part of the Red Roses' professional contracts. But even if I had cover, there was always the question about how it would affect my selection. Taking a year off at the peak of my career with a World Cup on the horizon didn't seem like an option, even though I felt my biological clock ticking. How do you keep going as an elite rugby player if you decide to take a break to focus on having a family? It's a question I know all professional female athletes at the top of their game must have to ask themselves. It formed part of my decision around when to retire, particularly once I passed the age of thirty. I wanted to focus on having a child – I was worried I would miss the boat.

After I retired, my relationship with Marcella started and, thankfully, she was also keen to start a family as quickly as possible following our engagement. As a same-sex couple, we had to investigate the next steps, which was fertility treatment. It was a big decision as there were significant financial costs to it, without any guarantees. We were fortunate to be in a position to pay for it, but it made me aware of how tough the process must be for those couples going through fertility treatment who are struggling financially to cover the cost. We also had to decide who was going to carry first. We agreed I would do it, but felt the pressure of making sure it was a success. Our first treatment was intrauterine insemination, which involves sperm being injected into the uterus, where they are left to fertilise the eggs naturally.

I had to wait two weeks before taking a pregnancy test to see if it had been successful. I was told to get on with my life as normal. I could go to the gym, I could go to work and socialise with my friends.

Two weeks normally flies by, whether you're working or on holiday. But waiting for a pregnancy test? It was the most agonising wait of my life. I could almost hear every second slowly tick by. And every thought went through my head. Don't move this way or that way in case it affects the egg being implanted. Every stressful thought you could imagine. When the two weeks had passed, we woke early and did the test. I had to pee on it and if a smiley face appeared on the stick, I was pregnant. If a sad face appeared . . . well, you guessed it. For something so serious, it seemed a crass process.

Unfortunately, the result produced a sad face. And boy were we sad. We both felt broken, and this was only our first attempt. It doesn't matter who you are or why you require fertility treatment, you pin all your hopes on the first attempt. We'd been realistic enough to know that there had been no guarantees, but it still hurt. I wasn't used to failing in life but looking at that pregnancy test, I felt like a failure.

It is an expensive process, but we decided to try again as we were desperate to have a child. I had to wait for a month to pass before having another attempt. Those agonising two weeks passed again. This time we got a different pregnancy test, perhaps hoping we would get a different result. We did, but not the one we wanted. I did the test around four in the morning. The result wasn't clear. The blue that was supposed to indicate if I was pregnant was faint. Was I pregnant or not! Not knowing was the worst result of all. Marcella jumped in her car. 'I'm going to get you another test,' she had told me. Fair play. I don't know how she managed to find one at that time in the morning, but she did. She came back with a digital one this time. I took the test again. This time it was clear. It was a SMILEY FACE! Our emotions had gone from despair to elation, an emotional rollercoaster that culminated in tears of joy.

Of course, as any parents will tell you, the positive test is only the start of the agonising journey to childbirth. If I'd thought the two-week wait had been tough, I seemed to spend the next nine months constantly worrying about the baby. At the twelve-week mark, we were at least able to start to tell people, and we felt a bit more at ease. But there were so many moments when I feared the worst. Without getting too graphic, I bled a lot and had to be rushed into hospital on a couple of occasions, fearing that it was a miscarriage. I was told that some women do bleed during pregnancy without having a miscarriage, but it was so stressful. I can remember trying to read the doctor's face when she came into the room to see if she looked like it would be good or bad news.

And to make it worse, the times I had to go to hospital were during the Covid pandemic, so I had to go alone. Marcella wasn't allowed to come in with me. In fact, she hadn't been allowed with me for any appointments. At the twelve-week scan, when I saw the foetus for the first time, then at the twenty-week scan to look for any abnormalities and when I was able to find out the sex of our baby. 'Thankfully everything is fine and you are going to have a boy,' the doctor told me. It was a moment I would love to have shared with Marcella, but instead I had to wait until I got to the car in the hospital carpark to tell her. It was a strange and challenging time. I've spoken to a lot of parents since who had 2020 babies and we shared a similar, lonely experience. We had to go through the pregnancy months without the social support from National Childbirth Trust classes, and at times without the face-to-face support of friends and family. I certainly had to go through some scary moments, when Marcella was stuck outside, waiting in the car.

But by October our beautiful baby boy, Artie, arrived. I'd trained right up until his due date. In the morning I did baby yoga, went to the shops and then watched *Tipping Point* on ITV – I love Ben Shephard. I had no idea what a contraction felt like, but it was while watching *Tipping Point* that I suddenly felt like I needed to go to the toilet, but at the same time didn't need to go to the toilet. Marcella looked it up on Google. 'You're having a contraction!' she exclaimed. Everything moved very quickly. We went to Stoke Mandeville hospital. I was in agony but was told that I was not fully dilated so could not stay unless I was moved to the ward and Marcella wasn't allowed to join me. So we went to a nearby Travelodge and, as I walked through the doors of the hotel, my waters broke. We rushed back to the hospital and a few hours later Artie was born. Thankfully Marcella was able to join me once I'd gone into labour. I proudly posted a picture of him on Twitter: 'I thought playing rugby for ENG was hard, but childbirth has to be the toughest thing ever!!! Thanks to the staff at Stoke Mandeville for looking after us,' I wrote.

The hospital treated me to the nicest tea and toast I have ever tasted and then the next day we were out in the world on our own, with a baby, waiting for someone to tell us what to do next! It was just us now, baby Artie.

Once we'd taken Artie home, I realised everything had changed. We both had the pressure now of wanting to raise him as best as we possibly could. I had thought rugby was the be-all and end-all, but being a parent felt so much more important and fulfilling.

After a year and half, we decided to try for number two, and this time Marcella decided that she would carry but use my eggs through IVF treatment, where the egg is removed from the woman's ovaries and fertilised with sperm in a laboratory. The fertilised egg, called an embryo, is then returned to the woman's womb to grow and develop.

We had a very tough time. It took several rounds of treatment, which was more invasive, and required a lot of medication.

Marcella sadly miscarried after one attempt. But then, after our fourth attempt, we were successful. It was such a relief to both of us and our families, who had been through the tough times with us. Thankfully Marcella had a much smoother pregnancy than I had. She said she actually enjoyed the nine months. Her due date was supposed to be around Christmas time. She held on long enough for us to have a nice Christmas dinner, but we decided against planning anything for New Year's Eve. Just as well. This time she needed to go to the toilet, but also didn't, so we headed back to Stoke Mandeville hospital again. The thought crossed our mind that our second baby could be the first newborn of 2023 if she arrived in the early hours of the morning. Another lady next door was also in labour, and the midwife started to play us off against each other. Marcella had more important things to concentrate on, but it was strange this time being the other partner. I got to understand what it must be like for fathers when their wives or partners are giving birth. You feel a bit helpless. I knew what she was going through in terms of the pain, anxiety and stress and it's really hard to see your loved one having to go through that. I tried to give her advice and support her. But at one point I fell asleep because I felt so tired. And I was only observing!

The same medical staff who were there for the birth of Artie were working that night, which was nice. 'Hi Maggie, great to see you, how are you doing?' said one of them. Knowing them all made the experience more comfortable for both of us and Marcella gave birth to our daughter, Willow, in the early hours of New Year's Day. What a special birthday! We feel like we have a strong family now, one boy and one girl. Who knows, there might be baby number three at some stage. Sometimes we joke about having a sevens team of our own.

People sometimes ask me what the greatest moment of my life has been. Was it winning my first cap? Or winning the World Cup? I can honestly say that following the arrival of Willow, considering the journey we'd been on, and how tough it had been, was *the* moment (alongside giving birth to Artie!).

I cried and cried. I have my own family now. I'm just so grateful because I know that some people are not able to have children, which had been a concern throughout my career. I know a lot of female athletes have the same dilemma. I just hope I can be as good a mum as mine has been for me. I'm so proud of the boy Artie is becoming and seeing Willow's personality come through is beyond rewarding. Our family unit strengthens more every day and I'm filled with hope and excitement for what the future will hold for us.

TWENTY-THREE

REBEL WITH A CAUSE

The day that I walked out of my job with the RFU and sat in the Starbucks near Twickenham station back in 2012, my overriding emotion had been one of relief. I was free of the toxicity and free to focus fully on playing for England again. Yet in my elation, I also made a vow to myself that one day I would go back and try to change the system from within.

It hadn't been possible to do so as an employee who was still trying to pursue a playing career for England. But one day, I said to myself, one day I would find a way back. I owed that much to the girls and women who were following in my footsteps.

I knew it would most likely have to be a long game. I knew nothing about RFU politics. My only reference point to the governing body's council was the remark made by former England captain Will Carling when he described it as a body of 'fifty-seven old farts' in a Channel 4 documentary broadcast on the eve of the 1995 Rugby World Cup.

Carling's comments cost him his captaincy, briefly, until a united squad demanded that he be reinstated before they set off for South Africa. Almost exactly twenty years later, I would receive an invitation to join the RFU council from one of Carling's old teammates, Jason Leonard, sitting in the Royal

Box at Twickenham, where the revolt at his dismissal had taken place.

As an ambassador for the 2015 World Cup, I was attending one of the England pool stage matches when I bumped into Jason, who was RFU president at the time, and he raised the idea. 'Have you ever thought about joining the RFU council?' he asked. 'There are two national members posts on the council, which are held by former England players to provide a past players' voice.' At the time they were held by Phil Vickery and Richard Hill, but he explained that Vickery was stepping down, so there was going to be a vacancy coming up. 'If you're interested it would be really good to have a different perspective, and being a former England women's player, you'd add value.' No one really used the terms diversity and inclusion back then, but I knew what he meant. There were barely any women members on the council, and certainly no people of colour. You would be hard-pressed to find many under the age of sixty either.

I thanked Jason for thinking of me for the role and told him I'd have a think and get back to him. I didn't have to think for too long.

If I knew very little about the council, I knew this was the moment for me to seize the opportunity to make a difference, to affect change. If I wanted to be a visible leader, this was a golden opportunity to join what was overwhelmingly a white and male governing body to blaze a trail not only for the women's game but for all people from ethnic minorities and those from less privileged backgrounds. I had initially thought that I could only make a difference by leaving the RFU. But change would only come from within.

I told Jase that I was interested, and he said he would start the ball rolling. I had to formally apply to become a 'national member' and then face an interview by the RFU's nominations committee. If my application was approved, the committee would then put my name up to a vote by the full council. It was a crash course in rugby governance. As a player I had never really understood what went on behind the scenes and like many other players I was naive to the inner workings of rugby politics. I can remember after certain England matches, our team manager Jan Man would say that some RFU council members were in attendance. But most of us didn't know what the RFU council was, never mind who was on it.

I like to be prepared, so I started to do my own research. I spoke to various people to find out more about the council and its workings. What attracted me is that standing for the council could give me a role in rugby that was not as a player on the pitch, or as a pundit from the sidelines, but would allow me to truly understand sports governance and help shape the future of our game through conversations, debate and being part of the decision-making process.

Thankfully the manner of my departure as an RFU employee didn't affect my application. In June 2016 I became the first former England Women's player to become an elected national member of the council and the only person of colour.

It felt like a small but historic step. I thought back to my pathway as a player. When I first started playing at Saracens, the England captain was Paula George, who is mixed-race, and she would be succeeded by one of my club teammates, Maxine Edwards, who is black. Seeing that Paula was the captain of the England team when I started out in rugby was a huge draw to me at a time when I could have committed to other sports. I'd seen myself reflected in rugby and rarely experienced racist issues while playing, except when travelling overseas.

By joining the sixty-one-strong RFU council, I could not only provide a voice for the next generation, but also provide them with visible leadership. I wanted everyone to see that rugby could be the game for them. I wanted to reach the inner cities and communities where there are a high number of black or Asian people and people with different faiths. Young people can be inspired by looking up and seeing people who look like they do and have similar types of background, just as I found Paula and Maxine inspirational figures.

****

My first mission was to find a blazer that fitted me. Yes, I was officially a *blazer* now (sorry, Will!). Deborah Griffin had represented women's rugby on the RFU council since 2010, but it wasn't until 2013 that Tracy Edmundson became the first woman elected to serve on one of the RFU constituent bodies as one of two representatives for Notts, Lincs and Derbyshire. So, let's just say the RFU did not have any female jackets available at the time, so I was sent a men's blazer. It hung on me like a tent. I had to get it cut to fit me, but it was so over-sized that it still didn't fit. Thankfully the RFU do now have female-cut jackets and we're given scarves rather than ties. But in 2016, it was a case of make do and mend.

Despite my grand ambitions, I felt anything but inspirational at my first council meeting. I didn't know what to expect. It was held in the Live Room at Twickenham stadium. I'd spoken to a few people about the etiquette, but my preparation did nothing to ease my anxiety.

The room was set up with lots of small tables forming one big rectangle. 'Don't be afraid to sit where you want,' someone told me. 'Some council members like to sit in the same place at every meeting and beside who they want to. Just don't let yourself be pushed into sitting somewhere else.'

I ended up sitting beside John Spencer, one of the legendary figures on the council, a former England and Lions centre, and former RFU president. He was charming and relaxed. I was still fraught with nerves.

I was also told that if you want to ask or answer a question you must raise your hand, wait for the president to acknowledge you, then use the microphone to speak and always start by stating my name first and then my council title (mine being National Member). This was to aid the minutes taken during each meeting. I was sent council papers to read through before the meeting to make sure I knew what was going to be discussed so I could contribute to the debate. For my first meeting, for some reason I had almost expected it to be like when new MPs in the House of Commons attend their first session and get to deliver a maiden speech, but it wasn't the case.

I didn't know if I was even allowed to speak in my first meeting. I would have loved to have formally introduced myself to everyone, stated my ambition and what I hoped to achieve in my time on the council and partnership with this group, but the council already had my biography and knew me as an England player (although there has always been more to me than the person you see on the playing field). I should have just said something straight away and taken control of the situation. 'Hello, I'm Maggie Alphonsi, I am honoured to be the new national member on the council and feel very proud to represent our members. I cannot wait to make an impact in helping to grow our great game and striving to make it a sport that is truly for all regardless of gender, ethnicity, sexuality, faith, disability or class. I want people to feel it is a game for them. It was this great game that saved my life and I believe everyone should be given the same opportunities to experience it and progress within it whatever role they choose to undertake. I am fully committed to this cause, and I am looking forward to working with each and every one of you to achieve this goal,' is what I should have said.

Own your voice, Maggie, *own your voice.* But I sat in silence, feeling with every passing minute that my moment to introduce myself had passed and growing concerned that if I asked for the microphone, there was a risk I would say something stupid, and was worried that every contribution was being minuted.

My confidence and standing on the council were given a timely boost, when in November 2016 I was inducted into World Rugby's Hall of Fame, along with several legends of the men's game including Jonny Wilkinson, Lawrence Dallaglio, Jeremy Guscott, Brian O'Driscoll, Shane Williams, the late John Dawes, as well as my great Canadian rival Heather Moyse at a ceremony at the Rugby Art Gallery, Museum and Library in Rugby, Warwickshire. It was a night to remember at which I was generously described as 'The First Lady of English women's rugby'.

At the second RFU council meeting I finally broke my silence, after an embarrassing number of seconds fumbling with the microphone. I can't even remember what I said, but in a way it didn't matter. I had found my voice. It would only grow. I had spoken once, and I knew I could do it again. It was as if I was a new member of a team. I was never one to walk straight into a dressing room and start mouthing off and upset people. I was the player who would stay quiet at first, look at and listen to my teammates until I understood who the key influencers in the squad were, and the dynamics of the interactions. Once I had enough information and context, then my confidence would grow to the point where I could first contribute and then start to speak my mind, then criticise and then lead. I hoped to be able to serve the full nine years that is allowed and felt I could make more of an impact by gaining the confidence of fellow council members first.

I vowed to myself that I would no longer be a spectator. I went on to sit on a number of committees, including the rugby growth subcommittee, which was all about identifying strategies to grow the game and support those from low socioeconomic backgrounds; the player development committee, which is about talent pathways; the community game board, which is a hugely influential group that sits underneath the main RFU board; and the diversity and inclusion implementation group, which is tasked with improving diversity and inclusion in the leadership within the community game.

At the start, almost all the conversations were about the men's game, with just the odd reference to the women's game, let alone diversity. It was often hard to be the only person of colour in the room because I felt that if I brought up certain issues, it could be difficult to get support or momentum. And if we did things around the women's game, then we didn't progress the conversation to also discuss race. Gradually more women came on to the council and the next person of colour was appointed, Tom Ilube, as chair of the RFU.

Jeff Blackett, the former RFU president, board member and disciplinary officer, and Genevieve Glover, chair of the diversity and inclusion implementation group, were also instrumental in co-opting four members to the council. All four have been a welcome addition and bring skills, knowledge and expertise to the council that goes beyond their age, gender, race and sexuality.

It has been a learning journey for me and the council and there has been a real desire for change. That was behind my decision to stand to become the president of the RFU. People who question my motives forget that I didn't even want to be an RFU council member at the start, never mind stand to become president. I felt I could make my biggest impact by putting my name forward in 2022 in order to become president for 2025 (you have to serve a year as junior and then senior vice-president before becoming president) to coincide with England hosting the women's Rugby World Cup.

The RFU council room at Twickenham features portraits of all the past presidents. Sadly, there was little variation between them – all were white men of a certain age, and many were from a privileged background. There wasn't a woman in sight, nor a person of colour. It lit my fire. I wanted to add a new face from a different background to that wall of presidents. If the UK government has had three female Prime Ministers, it was time for the RFU to have a female president at a time when the issues of diversity and inclusion have never been more relevant.

It has been so encouraging to see the England men's team feature more and more players from differing backgrounds. By 2023 around a third of the squad were players of colour. But we didn't see that reflected in the women's game. And then there were the leadership roles. The people who were making the decisions on the men's and women's games didn't fully reflect the members that played the game.

I looked up at those portraits and thought to myself: 'We need to change this.'

It was important to also have the right level of expertise, but I felt that I had that, otherwise I wouldn't have put myself forward. I also had a media profile that I felt would be a great platform to shout from the rooftops about just how great the sport of rugby is, and why the door was open for everyone to try it out.

It was fantastic to learn that two other women, Deborah Griffin and Gill Burns, the former England captain who had won the World Cup in 1994, had also put themselves forward to become junior vice-president. They both had long-standing commitments to the women's game and I vowed that if I didn't win the nomination, I would support either of them. It was fantastic that three strong female candidates went for the role.

I wanted to have an impact. I know that creating change is not about me. There have been tremendous strides forward taken by the women's game, but I also wanted to drive forward diversity in terms of race, sexuality, disability and faith. I want our game to *truly* be for all.

Following my application, I was interviewed by the standing nominations committee (they are the gatekeepers – they shortlist the applicants, interview them and decide who should be put forward for the council to vote on). I cannot go into details, but I didn't come out of the interview feeling particularly confident.

The first person I saw afterwards was Gill Burns, who said something really special: 'It doesn't matter who's successful. I know we will all support each other.' Her comment summed up the fantastic people in our game, and the women that I have played with and worked with. I loved that comment. It was exactly what I needed to hear in that moment.

I didn't make it to the second stage, but I vowed that I would give my full support to whoever was successful. The role wasn't about me, it was about the game and driving change. Yes, I felt frustrated and disappointed that I hadn't reached the next stage. Initially, I felt like I'd failed. All of those emotions of losing two World Cup finals and not making it as a shot putter all came flooding back. But then I stopped and reflected. Failure wasn't about getting the role or not, failure would have been not applying for the role in the first place. I'm glad I applied and made my intentions public. If you're not bold about your goals, then how will you ever create change?

Anyone who knows me should know that I never give up the fight, whatever the challenge may be. I've overcome the challenge of being born with the disability of a club foot, I have fought boys on the patch of ground at the back of my block of flats in Edmonton, I have tackled Owen Farrell, I have overcome the setback of being dropped by England after my first cap, come back from serious injury, the gut-wrenching disappointment of losing two World Cup finals before winning it on the third and final attempt and I have endured vitriolic racist and sexist abuse for daring, as a black gay woman, to have an opinion about rugby on television.

Missing out on the opportunity to be president at the women's World Cup in England in 2025 doesn't mean I have given up my hope that one day there will be a portrait of a person of colour on the wall of the RFU council room at Twickenham. At least, finally, there will be a woman up there in 2025 and I am pleased it will be Deborah Griffin OBE. An original member of the 'Fantastic Four' (the four women who started the Women's Rugby World Cup) who has done so much for our game.

My experience on the RFU council has revealed to me that I really do enjoy governance, something I admit I knew nothing about as a player. I love trying to make a difference by listening to the experiences of those around me. Maybe missing out on the opportunity to become junior vice-president was meant for a reason. It's making me look at other ways that I feel I can make a difference. I also sit on the Saracens board, and on an advisory group for Sporting Equals, alongside being a director at Vitality (the health insurers).

In the moments of doubt, or if I'm facing racist or sexist abuse on social media, when I am trying to influence change, I have my thirteen-year-old self at the back of my mind and how I overcame adversity and found the sport which saved my life. It's what drives me on every day: to think there are other boys and girls out there from a similar background to me who might be going through challenging times, but with the right support network they could find their sport or passion, which could change the course of their lives. It's why I strive to be a visible leader, to show what is possible, like Denise Lewis did for me when I saw her on TV all those years ago.

People ask me what keeps me motivated to stay in the game. It's because we haven't got equality and we haven't got parity. I keep asking myself why rugby is not more diverse when I know the talent is out there. I found the game and I loved it and was able to flourish in it. I have looked at other sports and wondered why some are more successful than others at encouraging and promoting diversity. Rugby is said to be a game for all shapes and sizes, so why not race, gender, sexuality and faith too? My goal is to push rugby to the masses. I might not always be able to do that through rugby governance, but by being a visible face on TV or through my column in the *Daily Telegraph*. I absolutely love it when people come up to me and say they're big fans of mine not because of what I did on the pitch but from seeing me talk about the game on media platforms, such as *BBC Breakfast*, *Good Morning Britain* or *Morning Live*. My goal is to one day appear on the BBC Radio 4's *Desert Island Discs* so listeners associate me with something other than just rugby – that will be when I feel I will have broken through.

The journey to become RFU president will be tough, but even though I have missed out on 2025, I'm not going to give up. And even if I don't make it, I have paved the way for someone else to do so. One of the things that I have learned through my leadership journey is that leadership is bigger than you; it's about the people around you and helping them to realise their potential so they can either follow or exceed your footsteps.

I recently have become good friends with a female rugby player called Zainab Alema, a black Muslim mother of three who has quit her nursing job and defied cultural expectations in order to pursue her dream of playing for England and becoming the first Muslim woman to do so. She also proudly wears a hijab and her drive and commitment to achieving her goal motivate me so much. We have an informal mentoring relationship. She gives me updates on where she is at, and I try to give her support and advice. What a fantastic ambition. I'm so pleased she's made her intentions public; she has put herself out there, and others will see her journey and will also be inspired by it.

When I put myself forward to be RFU president, I received quite a lot of racist abuse. But do you know what? If nothing else, putting myself forward to be president, some people now know that such a position at the RFU actually exists! And they now know what you have to do to apply for it and the successive roles you have to occupy before you become president. Jason Leonard was the last high-profile player to hold that role and he really brought it to people's attention and did a great job in the role. But I want to take the game of rugby union to people who haven't even heard of Twickenham, never mind the process of becoming president of the RFU.

I want to share with people that there are roles in grassroots rugby clubs that people can fulfil even if they don't or haven't ever played the game. You can be a treasurer or a social secretary at rugby club or take up a position on your constituent body committee, or become a council member. There are so many leadership roles out there, and my goal is to show as many people as possible that there are a plethora of options in which someone can get involved in our wonderful sport to grow it.

People talk about 'woke' culture and that people from ethnic minorities are only put in certain positions to tick a box. And I know that's what a lot of people who don't know me probably think about me, but I have to brush it off. I can't let that negativity in otherwise I'll start to believe it. Well, I am continuing my work with the RFU because I know I can do it, I have experience and I can bring something new to the role. I sometimes have to remind people that I have a goal and I am an expert in other areas other than a broadcaster. I had to prove that I was capable of becoming a broadcaster and was not just on television because I was a black woman. Now I have to prove to some that I'm not just on the RFU council because I'm a broadcaster.

When I consider everything that I gave up to play for my country, it's hard not to be offended when I am subjected to abuse. I can still remember running out for my first cap for England, standing proudly for the anthems and seeing an English flag in the crowd and thinking to myself, I was born and raised here, and do you know what, I would die for this country, that is how much I valued the flag and what the nation meant to me. So when I read on social media people telling me to go back to where I came from, I can only smile. *Are you having a laugh?* I know they're a small minority, and I shouldn't even give them the time of day, but it is hard at certain times not to let their poisonous words affect you.

But when I see so many women and people of colour working in broadcasting in other sports, I like to think I'm part of a generation of trailblazers who aren't going to be held down or stopped because people think differently about them. The negativity spurs me on to keep going. The one thing I can promise you is that I am not going to fade away.

I would like to leave you with one last quote. It has been said by many powerful women in history, but I have paraphrased Kamala Harris, the first female and person of colour to be elected Vice-President of the United States of America.

She said: *'I may be the first . . . but I won't be the last.'*

I hope my story has inspired you to realise your potential and never stop moving forward. Thank you for joining me on this journey.

ACKNOWLEDGEMENTS

Firstly, I would like to pay a huge thank you to Gavin Mairs for writing this book with me. I really appreciate the time, effort, and commitment he gave to helping me tell my story.

Gavin is a highly respected sports journalist and had to cope with the sad loss of his mother, Joyce, during the project but kept going, determined to finish the book as his tribute to her. Joyce had also been born in Edmonton, where I grew up, and she had taken a keen interest in my story when the book was first proposed. I felt a real connection with her, and it meant the world to me to know that she wanted my story to be told too.

Through numerous enjoyable chats, we managed to piece together the key moments of my journey, bringing out the most interesting elements. Gavin has presented the words that hopefully provide not only an entertaining story but also one which others can learn lessons from. I hope my experiences will inspire others to achieve their own goals. Thank you, Gav, it has been a pleasure working with you.

The book would not have happened without Julia Hutton, my agent, friend, and confidante. It was Julia who first came up with the idea of writing an autobiography and worked tirelessly to make it happen, sowing the seeds for the project during the Covid lockdown in 2020.

I first got to know Julia when she was the communications manager at the RFU with the England Women's team. At times it felt like she was my teammate too such was her support and passion to grow the profile of women's rugby. She became my agent shortly after I retired, setting up her own public relations and talent management company. I was proud to be her first client; it was the start of a wonderful partnership and friendship. Julia's support has encouraged me to establish a career in the media and to give leadership talks.

And if it wasn't for her drive and support to make this project work, it may never have happened. Jules, you are a legend and a pioneer for promoting women in sport. I am so pleased to see your company go from strength to strength.

It was Nick Walters, the literary agent at David Luxton Associates, who had the task of turning the concept into a reality, and his dedication and professionalism were key in finding us the right publisher, and I am so grateful to Peter Burns and his excellent team at Polaris Publishing for backing this idea and taking it to print. It was humbling to see Pete's commitment to getting my story out there, making sure it was published in such a high-class and professional manner.

A very special thanks must also go to Dominic Silvester, for investing in this project and believing in Gavin and me to bring this story to light. He has shown great passion and commitment to ensure stories like mine are told and act as an inspiration for others to overcome their personal battles in sport and life. His passion for rugby also goes back a long way, first investing in Saracens in 2002 and has been a board member ever since, eventually taking ownership of the club in 2021. Dominic has also been on the committee of the Cape Town-based Make a Difference Leadership Foundation (MAD) since 2003. The MAD foundation identifies, supports, and develops future leaders in the country by offering scholars assistance through mentoring and personal, academic and leadership development. He has been a huge backer of other people's book and I really value the fact that he wanted to support mine. Thank you, Dominic.

There are so many people who have helped me in my journey from a rebellious teenager who first found a focus and purpose through rugby and then through Saracens, the England Academy to finally to becoming a World Cup winner in 2014. There are too many to mention individually (but please know I am eternally grateful to each and every one of you), but I want to thank Liza Burgess, who first introduced me to rugby and believed in me at a point when my life could have gone in a different direction. Jo (Josena) Walker, my former head of year at school, was another who taught me to believe in myself. Not only did she invest in my first rugby tour but also taught me invaluable lessons in character and leadership (along with the support of my other PE teachers, Graham Webber and Louise Canty).

Katie Ball, my first coach at Saracens, followed by Amanda Bennett, have both been inspirational figures in my rugby journey, while Gary Street and Graham Smith showed faith in me through the tough times as well as the great ones with England. Both were more than just coaches to me, more like father figures. They were a shoulder to lean on during times of challenge on and off the field and I will forever be in debt to them for that. Thank you to my former teammates (and the management staff, especially Jan Man!) at Saracens and England, it was a pleasure to experience the highs and lows with you all. I will never forget the memories we created and I will forever cherish those friendships. We have a bond that can never be broken.

Thank you to Ali Oliver, Dame Sue Campbell and Shaun Marsden-Heathcote at the Youth Sport Trust for helping me realise my potential and enabling me to thrive in the workplace. Thanks to Nick Reed and Neville Koopowitz at Vitality, for giving me a chance and never failing to show your continued support and encouragement.

To the Rugby World Cup winning coach, friend and ally, Sir Clive Woodward. I am blown away by your kind words. You and Jayne have always championed my achievements and provided good advice to me when needed. Clive, I am so pleased that you were able to contribute to the book and be part of a story that needs to be told.

Above all, I could not have achieved anything without the love and support of my family. My mum dedicated her life to not only give me the best start in life that she could but also supported me unfailingly in moments of adversity and, surprisingly, even fell in love with rugby too. She enabled me to become the person I am today.

The unstinting support of my wife Marcella has also given me the confidence to keep striving to make a difference, even in the face of the barbs on social media, to improve equality for women and those from ethnic minorities and from less privileged backgrounds. Marcella is not only my best friend but also my pillar of strength.

My two children, Artie and Willow, are our inspiration, and I look forward to seeing them both grow up to become caring, responsible and loving people. I must also send big love also to my two dogs, Nala and Tinker, and my first dog Muffin, who is sadly no longer with us but not forgotten.

Finally, I would like to thank you, the reader, for taking an interest in my story and showing support for a female athlete. This book is for all those I hope will follow in my footsteps and even go one step further and exceed them.